JELLY-BELLY

THE MACHO SERIES BOOK FOUR

KAY ELLIS

ENCOMPASS INK

CONTENTS

CHAPTER 1

I'M NOT A NICE PERSON. That's the first and last thing anybody needs to know about me. I mean, I must have been nice once, right? As a kid? I don't remember. It wasn't even as though I could blame my parents. They'd done their best. Both of them had worked full-time jobs so that we could have things like family holidays, and I always had a bike and the latest toys. They were still married. To each other too, which was more than you could say for most of my friends' parents. My mum and dad had accepted my sexuality, although I didn't think me coming out as gay when I was fifteen had come as any great surprise to them or anyone else. Which didn't go to say they were happy about it, but at least they hadn't kicked me out and disowned me like some I knew. It wasn't their fault I hardly ever went home to see them. It was mine. Like I said – I'm not very nice.

No, unfortunately, there was nobody to blame for my dubious personality other than myself. For whatever selfish reason, I seemed unable to stop using and abusing people, pushing away anyone stupid enough to actually give a damn about me. I'd loved, but never been in love. Maybe with

Stefan, but that was different. He'd been my best friend since secondary school. By the time I realised my feelings for him went beyond friendship, it was too late. The lines of our relationship had been drawn and it would have been weird for me to cross them. Besides, Stefan had never looked at me that way, and he'd left me too, once he met and fell in love with my arch-nemesis, Alex-bloody-Gill.

Then there was Eric. The rejection was still fresh with that one. I thought I loved him, but it turned out what I really loved was the security he provided. Or, in other words – his money. Eric was lovely, but he was also a pushover. He paid my rent and all my bills, he put food in the cupboards and credit on my phone. He loaned me his car whenever I asked for it and bought me clothes and Xbox games. Admittedly, he hadn't always known about the latter. He'd give me money for groceries and I'd see a nice pair of jeans or boots or a newly released game before I got as far as the supermarket.

Like an idiot, I'd chucked him out after a stupid argument. I thought he'd come back, grovelling and begging for a second chance, because – let's face facts – he loved me more than I ever did him. Instead, he'd met Mason White, who turned out to be a rich and famous rock star. Eric hadn't looked back. He'd gone to America with Mason and, just like that, my meal ticket was gone. To add insult to injury, Mason looked way too much like Alex Gill for my liking. Personally, I could never understand the attraction for musclebound meatheads.

My friends were all like me. Small, slim, stylish twinks. Stefan hated that word. *Twinks*. Why deny what we were though? I wasn't ashamed to call myself that.

What I was ashamed of was having to get a job as a waiter in a local Italian restaurant, now that I had to pay my own way. Killigan insisted on it. I'd been staying with him and Marcie ever since Eric left and I lost the flat. Marcie was an absolute angel, who wanted nothing more than to mother me to death. Something I could have lived with quite easily, only Killigan said otherwise. He'd gone out and found me a job without even asking. A favour from a friend, he'd said. Basically, the message had been 'get to work or get out', which was totally unfair, because when Stefan left Alex and came to stay with us, he spent all day in his room staring out of the window and nobody told him he had to get a job.

So – work it was, even if the uniform was horribly bland and unfashionable. The owner, Franco, was okay, but his bitch wife, Alison, seemed to have a problem with me. She wouldn't let me wear make-up or dye my hair anything other than brown. The pinks, blues and purples I'd sported in the past were now only a temporary thing for nights out.

My work colleagues were not exactly my type of people either. For a start, they were all straight. Stuart was a typical twenty-something, who talked about football, nights out on the lash and banging his bird, in that order. Then there was Jamie, who was at university. I had no idea what he was studying, mainly because I'd never bothered to ask. Alison liked to tell the rest of us that Jamie was the only one of us who would ever amount to anything. What we all knew and she didn't, was that he turned up stoned for practically every shift and had to sleep it off in the store room while the rest of us covered for him. Oh, and he also gave regular free-bies to his mates. If Alison was nicer to us, we might have told her what Boy Wonder was really like. She wasn't though, so we didn't.

Last, but by no means least, there was Landon. I got the impression that, like me, he had been taken on as a favour, probably because no one else would hire him. Landon was massively overweight. I mean, the guy was huge, to the point that when he walked, everything jiggled. Belly, thighs, fat arse... *everything*. Even so, he was probably the best of the bunch. He kept himself to himself and worked hard, even if he was a bit awkward and slow.

My friends came into the restaurant too some nights, a group of bitchy queens whose lives and relationships were every bit as shallow and meaningless as mine. I knew they'd cottoned on to the fact Jamie gave his mates free food, and they probably expected me to do the same for them. I needed this job though, and none of my friends were likely to offer to put a roof over my head if I got fired and Killigan kicked me out. Which was why I made sure they were seated in someone else's section. Nothing I could do about the bill then, right?

The mistake I made that night, was putting them in Landon's section. They were my friends though, at the end of the day, and I still wanted them to have good service. Jamie was so bombed he'd forget half their order, and Stuart would make obvious gay jokes and think it was okay because he added "no offense" on the end. I saw the way they looked at Landon though, when he waddled over to their table. Let's be honest, it was the same way I looked at him, with a mixture of derision and repulsion, but it was different when my friends did it. For reasons I couldn't explain, it bothered me more than I ever imagined it would.

My own tables were busy, but I tried to keep an eye on my friends at the same time. Looking out for them or for Landon? I wasn't sure I'd even decided that for myself. It was embarrassing though, the way they all bounced in their seats every time Landon lumbered past the table; how they puffed out their cheeks and held their arms out, in the universal sign language for "fat bastard". Then I heard them all fall about laughing when Louis dived under the table and yelled "Earthquake!" as Landon approached the table with the first of their meals.

Maybe I was coming down with something. I certainly felt sick, and something had to be wrong for me not to find the behaviour of my friends hilarious. Any other time, I'd be laughing with them, joining in with a few hilarious quips of my own. But this wasn't funny. It wasn't clever. It was just... *wrong*.

I put a plate in front of my customer with an apologetic smile. The couple, husband and wife I assumed, were close enough to Landon's table that they had to be hearing everything that was being said. From the pained expressions on their faces, the antics of their immediate neighbours were spoiling their evening as well as mine and Landon's.

"What happened to the rest of it?" Sebastian's overly loud voice echoed around the restaurant. Everyone, diners and waiters alike, stopped what they were doing to turn and stare. "Did you get hungry on your way from the kitchen?"

Louis and the others laughed like Seb had just said the funniest thing ever. I looked at Landon. His face was beetroot, his gaze fixed firmly on the floor. I'd noticed that about Landon. He didn't like to make eye contact with people.

"Th... that's the usual portion size," Landon mumbled.

"Are you sure?" Seb questioned. "Because it really does look as though someone has eaten half of it already. You look like you can't go for long with putting something in your fat mouth, so I have to assume it was you."

"No, I didn't... I wouldn't..."

"Well, I demand to see the manager," Seb said, looking around. "I'm not paying for some greedy, fat slob to pig out on my food before it gets to the table."

"Please..."

Landon's bottom lip trembled, and I could see he was close to tears. I still didn't know why I cared all of a sudden, but I hoped he didn't cry in front of them. Sebastian and Louis, they wouldn't remember this night in a couple of months' time. Landon would be just another guy they'd used to get a free meal. That's what we were all about, myself included. Make a fuss. Cause a scene. Get the meal fully comped by management who were usually keen to avoid any trouble. I'd done it myself on a number of occasions. No, they wouldn't remember the specifics, but being publicly reduced to a snivelling wreck would probably stay with Landon for the rest of his life.

"Seb, stop it," I said, too little too late.

Alison was bearing down on us, her expression ice cold as she glared at Landon. Obviously, she'd already decided that, whatever was going on, Landon was to blame.

"Is there a problem here, gentlemen?"

"Yes, there most certainly is." Seb indicated his plate and then looked at Landon. "I believe this jelly-belly has taken food from my plate."

Louis and the others snickered, while Landon seemed to shrink into himself, in as much as that was possible.

"Actually, Sir, I think you'll find that's our standard portion," Alison said with a tight smile. "However, I could speak to Chef and..."

"Porky's probably eaten him too," Louis said to another round of laughter.

Landon bolted. Saying he ran would be a gross exaggeration, but it was definitely a fast waddle. I hesitated for a moment, and then went after him. I mean, fuck knows why. What could I do to make anything better? And why did I even care? All I knew was, I had to try.

Outside, a light drizzle was falling. If I'd been wearing my own clothes, and my rather fabulous suede boots, I wouldn't have gone out there, but... hey, I was in my drab work clothes, and I really didn't give a shit if they got wet. Landon sat on the kerb, head hanging low. A cigarette dangled from his fingers, but he wasn't smoking it. I dropped down beside him, not entirely surprised when he refused to look at me.

"Is this okay?"

He shrugged. "Aren't you afraid I'm going to eat you?"

"You know what?" I tilted my head back, letting the soft rain fall onto my upturned face. "A few years ago, I probably would have thought exactly that." Landon turned his head to glare at me. "It's true," I continued. "For most of my teenage years, I had an eating disorder. I was border-line anorexic, the doctors said. I was trying to figure out who I wanted to be, I guess. It wasn't about being gay or straight or any other label people wanted to apply. I just wanted to be pretty, and to me, that meant being thin. Eventually, I realised it wasn't that I wanted to be a girl. I was just a boy who liked wearing make-up and nice clothes."

I coughed to clear the painful lump that had lodged in my throat. Why was I telling him any of this? I never talked about that confused period of my life to anyone. Not even Stefan, and he would swear blind he knew everything about me. He didn't. Not by a long shot.

"Anyway, the point is," I told Landon, "there was a time, when I was at my worst, that I couldn't bear to be around... well, *fat* people, because I genuinely believed they would eat me."

Landon was silent, like he was debating in his head whether or not he should believe me. In the end, he must have decided that he did. He tossed the cigarette butt into the gutter and twisted around to face me.

"How old were you?" he asked. His voice was low and soft for a man of his stature, as though he was unaccustomed to speaking to people all that often. Maybe that was the truth of it. Like I said, he kept himself to himself most of the time. "When you realised you were... you know."

"Gay?"

Landon nodded and looked away, but not before I saw the blush on his big apple-round cheeks.

"I don't know. I think I must have led a pretty sheltered life as a kid. I'd heard the word at school, like any other kid, but I didn't really understand what it meant. I knew I was different to the other boys though. I must have been thirteen when my problems started. I remember spending my whole birthday party crying because my cousin, Lucy, had a sparkly gold dress on and I was so jealous. But I didn't know then it was because I was gay. Like I said, I just wanted to be pretty."

"I was thirteen too," Landon said quietly. Wait, was he saying what I thought he was saying? Thirteen when he what exactly? "You think you had a sheltered life? You should try growing up in my family. Being gay was never an option."

"You're gay?" Okay, so he was saying it. Colour me surprised. "Wow, my gaydar must be well and truly broken. I had no idea."

"Why would you? You've never spoken to me before tonight."

I hung my head, knowing that what he'd said was the verbal equivalent of a bitch slap. It made me feel slightly ashamed that I'd never even tried to get to know him before, and that in itself was weird, because I didn't think I'd ever experienced shame before in my entire life. So, was I really that shallow? So self-absorbed that I wouldn't look twice at a guy because he was fat? If I didn't find a man attractive, he wasn't worth my time? Was that it?

"Anyway," Landon said, after an awkward pause. "When I realized I was... different, that I liked boys more than girls, I panicked. I stopped going out. Pushed away all my friends. Then, because I was bored and lonely, I started eating. After a while, I figured out that the bigger I got, the more I repulsed people. And that was a good thing, because it meant I was safe. My sinful, sexual orientation became irrelevant because nobody, male or female, was ever going to fancy me when I look like this."

He sounded so matter of fact about it. I felt sorry for him. Yeah, I'd been confused for a few years, there was no denying that, but I'd never had to hide who and what I was. Hell, not hiding it had gotten me beaten up and put in hospital more than once. I wasn't going to let it stop me dressing up and wearing make-up though. I couldn't imagine how it must feel to be Landon, forced to hide the truth beneath layers of fat and misery.

"You shouldn't say that," I said. "What we are isn't sinful."

"The bible says it is."

"Doesn't the bible also say that all men are created equal? If you believe in God, then you have to believe he made us this way. That this is his plan for us, right?"

"I don't know," Landon said miserably. "Maybe."

"And, for the record, you're not repulsive." It wasn't necessarily a lie. Just because I would never fancy a fat blob like him in a million years, it didn't mean someone else wouldn't be desperate enough to find him attractive. "You've got nice eyes."

Landon leapt to his feet with surprising agility for a man of his size.

"Don't tease me, Rufus. It's not nice and it's not fair."

"Wait, what did I say?"

He didn't answer, turning his back on me and walking away, leaving me sat in the rain and wonder what I'd done wrong.

CHAPTER 2

IT HAD GONE one in the morning by the time I got home. I'd returned to work after my talk with Landon, while he left early without finishing his shift. My friends had gone too by the time I went back into the restaurant, although I didn't know whether they left voluntarily or if Alison had thrown them out. I hadn't dared ask, not wanting to draw attention to the fact I knew them and would therefore be seen as guilty by association. Besides, Alison had been in a pissy mood for the rest of the night, having to cover both mine and Landon's tables herself when we pulled our disappearing act. She hadn't threatened to fire me though, which was the only positive to come out of the entire night.

Killigan was still up. He was working at the dining room table, paperwork spread out all over the place. I didn't know if policemen were supposed to bring their casework home, but whatever it was, it was taking all of his attention. He was totally absorbed, making notes on the legal pad in front of him. I dithered in the doorway for a moment, debating whether I should speak to him or not. He didn't like me, but then he didn't like Alex much either, so I tried not to take it personally. It was the only thing Alex and I had in common, other than the fact we were both in love with Stefan.

"Did you want something, Rufus?" Killigan didn't look up when he spoke. I almost jumped out of my skin, not even realising he knew I was there.

"Can I talk to you about something?"

He pointed with his pen to the chair opposite him. "So long as you're not going to tell me you lost your job. I meant what I said, Rufus. Either you work and pay your way, or you move out."

"It's nothing to do with work," I said, dropping into the chair. "Well, it is in a way, I guess, but not what you're thinking."

"Spit it out, Rufus. I haven't got all night."

"Am I a horrible person?"

Okay, that wasn't quite what I'd intended to say, but he said spit it out and for some reason those were the words that spewed forth when I opened my mouth. Killigan put his pen down and stared at me.

"Do you really want me to answer that?"

"No, don't bother." I picked at my thumb nail, feeling suddenly awkward. "I already know what you're going to say."

"Okay, listen." Killigan sighed. "You're not the easiest person to get along with, but I think you know that. The way you behave towards Stefan, Alex and Eric has been pretty shitty at times. I'm sure you know that too. You use people, Rufus, and you have to be the most selfish person I have ever met. I'm sorry, but that's the truth of it."

He sat back, waiting for an answer, but what was there to say? I couldn't deny a single word of what he'd said. And, what was that saying about the truth hurting? Man, did it ever. A tear escaped the corner of my eye and rolled down my cheek. I brushed it away quickly, refusing to give into self-pity for once.

"Tell me what's going on with you, Rufus," Killigan said, not unkindly. "Are you in some kind of trouble?"

"No." I shook my head and sniffed. "It's this guy at the restaurant - Landon."

"Which one is he?" Killigan asked. "The druggie, the fat one, or the one who thinks he's God's gift to women?"

"The fat one." I frowned. "But you shouldn't call him that. It's not nice."

"Okay, I apologise." Killigan raised an eyebrow at my comment and gave me a cynical look. I knew why. I was the queen of bitchy put-downs, and here I was telling him off for calling someone fat. "What about him?"

"There were some customers giving him a hard time about his weight." I left out the part about those customers being friends of mine, still feeling a sense of shame about it. "Landon got upset and I tried to make it better, but I think I only made things worse."

"I see. Why do you think you made it worse?"

"I wanted to make him feel better about himself, so I told him he had nice eyes."

"And has he? Got nice eyes, I mean?"

"Yeah, I guess so. They're big and brown, and he's got these really long eyelashes." Wow. Now I thought about it, I realised it was true. Landon Holby *did* have nice eyes. "He didn't believe me though. He thought I was teasing him, and he stormed off."

"I see," Killigan said again. he tapped his pen against the table and regarded me solemnly for a what felt like an age. I got the impression, that like Landon had before, he was trying to gauge just how serious I was being. "Why are you telling me this, Rufus?"

"Because I want to make things right," I told him, "and I don't know how."

"Will the real Rufus Haynes please stand up," Killigan muttered, under his breath, but I heard him anyway. He wasn't buying it. Didn't believe that I wasn't trying to manipulate him somehow, or that I had it in me to act like a halfway decent human being. He probably thought it was all part of some cruel plan to hurt either him or Landon. Maybe it was the copper in him, trained to be suspicious of my motives. I had form after all.

"Please, Killigan," I said. "Tell me what to do."

He sighed again. "You could try telling him you're sorry. That's always a good place to start."

"I tried." I let out a groan and dropped my head to rest it on the edge of the table. I may even have banged it against the wooden surface a couple of times for good measure. "See? This is why I'm such a fucking arsehole the whole time. I suck at being nice."

Killigan laughed and reached across the table to ruffle my hair. I jerked back in surprise. Marcie was always hugging me, but Killigan had never touched me before, certainly not with any modicum of affection.

"If you really mean it," he said, "tell him again. Keep telling him until he listens."

"I'll do my best." I got to my feet, tired, fed up, and ready to call it a night. "Thanks."

"Rufus." Killigan's stern voice stopped me in my tracks. "I don't know what game you're playing, but if you do anything to hurt this kid..."

He left the threat unspoken. I nodded to show I understood. How could I blame him for thinking the worst of me when that was all he had ever seen? I went up to my room and undressed before getting into bed naked. I lay down and close my eyes. An hour later, I was still awake, tossing and turning restlessly.

Eventually, I sat up with a frustrated growl. If this was what having a conscience felt like, then I wasn't so sure I wanted one. I'd managed without one for all these years. Why suddenly go getting one now? And why did it have to choose half past two in the morning to remind me that Landon was not the only person I needed to apologise to for my past behaviour?

I switched on the bedside lamp and reached for my phone. Without thinking about what time it was or – more likely – acting like a selfish prick again, I dialled my parents' number. Dad answered, sounding out of breath. I smiled slightly, imagining him running down the stairs and standing in the hallway in his vest and boxer shorts. They were old fashioned like that, my parents, still preferring a house phone to mobiles. I knew they both had mobiles, but they didn't use them often and switched them off before going to bed.

"Hi, Dad."

"Rufus? Do you know what time it is?"

"Yeah, sorry. I couldn't sleep."

"Is everything okay?" He sounded worried, which was understandable, I suppose, given the hour and the fact that I hardly ever called them for any reason other than to ask them to loan me money that I never paid back. "Wait there. I'll get your mother."

"No, Dad. I..."

I was wasting my breath. He'd already gone. I heard his distant, muffled voice as he shouted for my mother. A moment later I heard her answer him, her tone anxious as she came down the stairs.

"Rufus, sweetheart, what's wrong?" I held the phone

away from my ear, almost deafened by her near hysterical screech. Guess now I'd have to apologise for worrying them on top of everything else. "Hush, Jerry, I'm asking him. Darling, what's happened?"

"Nothing. Everything's fine, Mum. I shouldn't have called at this time. Go back to bed. I'll call you later."

"Rufus Bartholomew Haynes, don't you dare hang up on your mother."

"Wow. My full name. Really?"

"It's your own fault," she said. "You forced me into it. Now, tell me what's wrong. Are you sick?"

"Seriously, Mum, it's nothing. I just... I miss you. I was wondering if I could come and see you. Maybe next weekend?"

"This is your home, Rufus. You don't need to ask permission to visit. Only, we thought... well, to be honest, we thought you didn't want to see us anymore. It's been so long since you've been home."

"I know. I'm sorry." I rubbed a hand across eyes that were suddenly hot and blurry. "Saturday, though. I'll be there. I promise."

"Well, that's wonderful. Do you need money for the train?"

"Yeah, I..." She sounded so ridiculously happy that it only compounded my guilt further. "Actually, no. I've probably got enough."

I promised I would be there on Saturday and hung up. I'd just made my mother a promise I wasn't sure I would be able to keep. As yet, I didn't know if I could get the time off from the restaurant.

So, that made me a horrible person *and* a terrible son. I was a useless boyfriend as well.

A user, that's what Killigan called me, and he was right.

I'd taken Eric for every penny, and then sold him out for a few hundred quid more when Mason White had offered me cash in exchange for Eric's whereabouts. Eric had even signed his car over to me when he left for America and I had sold it two days later. That money had gone on clothes I wasn't sure I liked once I got them home, and a pair of incredibly expensive boots that were so uncomfortable I'd only worn them once.

So, Eric was next on my list.

I fired up my laptop, the one thing of any worth that I hadn't sold yet, and logged into Facebook. If I remembered correctly, the time zone where Eric currently lived was about five hours behind the UK. Eric's boyfriend, Mason, would still be on stage with his band and I had to assume Eric would be close by, in the auditorium if not in the wings. Mason had concocted some bogus job title to get Eric on the payroll, so he'd be there with the crew somewhere. *Sorry for everything,* I typed. Eric would get the message when he got back to hotel room or wherever it was they were staying.

Before I had the chance to log out again, my laptop pinged to alert me of an incoming message.

Sorry for what exactly? Are you okay?

Shit. I hadn't intended Eric to get my message and reply straight away. Now I'd probably be accused of trying to manipulate him somehow; of playing on his kind heart and trying to come in between him and Mason. A few weeks ago, I probably would have done just that, but I'd come to realise I didn't want Eric back anyway.

Thought you'd be at a show.

Tour doesn't start until next week. A pause and then: *You didn't answer. What's wrong?*

Why did something have to be wrong with me before I

could do anything nice? Was that really what people thought of me - that I had to have a terminal illness or something before I was capable of acting like a halfway decent human being? Well, of course it was what they thought. It wasn't as though I had ever given them any reason to think otherwise, was it?

Sorry, but I can't send you any more money if that's what you're after. Not after last time.

My gaze flickered guiltily to the jacket hung on the back of the bedroom door. Eric had sent money to cover my rent. Okay, I admit, I asked him to, but only because Killigan had been on my case about paying my way. I knew Eric had gone against his new boyfriend's wishes in doing so, but he'd sent me a couple of hundred. A loan, he'd called it, although we both knew I'd never pay him back. Anyway, the same day I got the money, Marcie told me she'd wait for her rent until I received my first month's wages from the restaurant. What else was I supposed to do, other than spend the money on the simply fabulous jacket I'd had my eye on for weeks and never imagined I'd be able to afford? I didn't know who'd told Eric that I'd abused his trust yet again, but my guess would be Killigan.

At least Eric was used to me letting him down. I'd done it enough times in the past. Used him. Stolen from him. Lied and cheated almost as a matter of habit. I didn't kid myself either. If he hadn't left me when he did, I'd have kept on doing all those things without any remorse whatsoever.

I'll pay you back, I messaged. I meant it too. Maybe not all in one go, because waiting tables didn't exactly pay big bucks, but I'd get there eventually. Besides, it wasn't like Eric needed the money now he was shacked up with a big, fancy-pants rock star. *Nothing wrong. Couldn't sleep.*

Wanted to say sorry for all the shit I did when we were together.

Okay, that's it. Now I know you're ill. Do I need to come home?

That was typical Eric. All I had to do was say the word and that bleeding heart of his would have him on the next plane home. The old me might have said yes, just for the Hell of it, but that wasn't who I wanted to be anymore. Added to which, the last thing I needed was his huge, rock-god boyfriend coming after me.

No, I'm fine. Just feeling sorry for myself.

We exchanged a few more messages, which mainly consisted of me convincing Eric that I wasn't on my death bed. Eventually, I told him I thought I'd be able to sleep. I closed my laptop, turned out the light and settled down, but still sleep did not come. My body refused to relax and my brain wouldn't switch off, churning over memories of every bad thing I'd ever done. For the first time in forever, I was taking a long hard look at myself, and to be honest I wasn't sure I liked what I saw.

CHAPTER 3

IT WAS late by the time I managed to drag myself out of bed. Tired and irritable, I plodded, barefoot, downstairs to the kitchen. Marcie stood at the counter making herself a late lunch. She looked up with a smile when I walked in.

"I'm having a sandwich," she said, waving a buttery knife at me as though she was proving her point. "Do you want one? Or I could cook you something. Bacon and eggs sound okay?"

I opened my mouth to accept and then remembered the promise I made myself to be a better person. This was my first day as the new and improved Rufus Haynes, which meant no more letting Marcie wait on me hand and foot. From now on, I was going to pull my weight around here, starting with making my own breakfast. Lunch. Whatever.

"I can do it," I told her, even though I had no idea where to begin.

When I was with Eric, we had take-out more often than not. Always at his expense, of course. Then I'd moved into Marcie's and been quite content to sit back and let her molly-coddle me.

"Oh, lovey," Marcie laughed, "we all know you can't do as much as boil an egg." She threw me a questioning look as she went to the fridge and began pulling out enough food to feed a small army let alone little old me. "Is this about Killigan? Has he been nagging you again?"

"No, it's not that." It always made me smile to hear Marcie call him Killigan. They'd been together for a little over two years now, since they met when Stefan and Alex were attacked, and I'd never once heard her call him by his first name. "Well, I mean... he always nags a bit." Make that a lot. "But it doesn't bother me. I just... you know... thought I could start helping out more around the house."

Marcie stared at me, frying pan in hand. I waited for her to launch into the whole *'Are you ill?'* routine. She didn't. Instead, she held up the pan with a smile.

"Would you like me to teach you to cook a few basic things?"

"You mean now?"

"It's as good a time as any. Come on. We can start with bacon and eggs."

I really wasn't in the mood for a cooking lesson, but Marcie had a way of making people want to please her. The woman had a kind and generous nature and would never knowingly do anything to hurt anyone. She called us her boys; me, Stefan and Alex. Eric too for a short while. Every single one of us would move Heaven and Earth to make her happy. And if that meant learning to cook bacon and eggs, then so be it.

In the end, much to my surprise, I had the most fun I'd had in ages. We didn't just stop at bacon and eggs either. Bread, biscuits and muffins followed, and the afternoon flew by. As we worked, we chatted and laughed, not about anything important, but Marcie was good company and, for once, I felt like I could be myself. No pretence. No airs and graces. This was the Rufus I was when there was nobody around to see. The one who didn't have an image to maintain. The one who could forget the carefully cultivated 'Rufus' image and just enjoy life. It had been a long time since I'd allowed that side of me out to play.

Killigan arrived home to find the two of us covered in flour, our hands sticky with chocolate. He watched us from the doorway, an amused look on his face.

"What's going on here then?"

"You're the detective. You work it out," Marcie laughed. "If you're looking for clues, you might want to examine the tray of chocolate chip cookies Rufus made. They're not long out of the oven, so they'll still be warm."

Killigan came further into the kitchen and eyed the tray of cookies dubiously. I didn't blame him. I wouldn't trust me not to poison him either.

"Rufus made these?"

"Yes, go on. Try one. They're really very good," Marcie encouraged. "The boy's a natural."

"You don't have to," I mumbled awkwardly as Killigan reluctantly plucked a cookie from the tray. "It's probably terrible."

"I'm sure it's fine," Killigan said.

He bit into the cookie. Closed his eyes. Sighed. He didn't like it. I couldn't help it. I was disappointed enough that I could have cried. All that hard work and effort and I couldn't even bake a stupid cookie properly.

"Sorry."

"Sorry?" Killigan's eyes sprang open and he looked at me in surprise. "What the Hell are you sorry for? Rufus, this has to be the best cookie I've ever tasted. It's bloody delicious."

He pushed the remainder of the cookie into his mouth in one go, before snagging another two from the tray. Disappointment was instantly replaced by a warm fuzzy feeling and just the smallest sense of pride.

"Told you," Marcie gloated. "He's a natural. A few more lessons and he'll be running the kitchen at Franco's."

Heat flooded my face and I turned away, unaccustomed to praise from anybody who wasn't saying it just because they wanted to go to bed with me. Most compliments I got were along the lines of *'you're-so-hot-I-wanna-fuck-your-brains-out'*. And, it wasn't even that I really was all that hot. More like I was incredibly easy and everyone knew it. Funny, but I never imagined that when I did find something I was good at outside of the bedroom it would be cooking. Working in the kitchen at Franco's wasn't the worst idea I'd heard. Sure, I'd have to start at the bottom, but it couldn't be any worse than waiting tables. I wondered if I should ask Killigan to have a word with Alison, or whether I should take the plunge and do it myself. No, not Killigan. If I really wanted this, it was down to me to sort it out, without relying on someone else to do the hard part for me. Wasn't that part of growing up?

"Talking of Franco's," I said, "I should get moving, I might go in early and talk to Alison about something."

"Don't even think about quitting," Killigan growled around a mouthful of crumbs. "I don't care how good your chocolate chip cookies are."

"I won't," I promised.

I went upstairs and dressed in my bland uniform of black trousers and white shirt. I mean, come on. Would a bit of colour really hurt? I had to toe the line though, especially if I was going to ask Alison for a favour.

If I was honest with myself, Alison wasn't the only

person I was hoping to see before my shift started. If I got the chance, I wanted to speak to Landon too. I didn't know why it mattered, but I needed him to believe that I hadn't been mocking him the night before. Okay, he might not be my type, but he *did* have nice eyes. They'd be even better if he ever went on a diet and they weren't so lost in his fat, puffy face.

Half an hour later, I arrived at the restaurant and any of thoughts of asking Alison for that favour went right out of my head. The front picture windows of the restaurant were plastered with dozens upon dozens of A4 sheets of paper. Stuart and Jamie were already there with buckets of soapy water, painstakingly peeling the posters from the glass. As I got nearer, I realised what was on them. Some of the pictures were of pigs, others of grotesquely fat men. All of them had words printed across them in bold capital letters. Mean and juvenile words like lard-arse and jelly-belly. Shit. That was the word my friends had used to insult Landon the night before. They wouldn't be so stupid as to vandalise the restaurant, would they? Or so vindictive? God, what would Landon think if he saw this crap spread across the windows of his workplace?

"You should be doing this," Stuart complained, giving me a sour look. "It was your mates who did this, after all."

"They wouldn't," I said, sounding so weak and pathetic I couldn't even convince myself. "They're not like that."

Part of me wanted to believe that Sebastian and the others didn't have it in them to do anything as ballsy as causing criminal damage, but that word... jelly-belly. Who else could it have been? It was too much of a coincidence for it to be anybody but them.

"I'll come and help in a minute," I told my scowling workmates. "I need to speak to Alison first."

I hurried through the restaurant and found Alison in her office. Unsurprisingly, she didn't exactly look pleased to see me. Fuck, was I going to lose my job over this? Killigan would kick me out and then what was I supposed to do? It wasn't even my fault. If anything, it was Landon's own stupid fault for being so fat he attracted the wrong kind of attention.

Annnnd...way to go, Rufus. First day of being the new and improved me and I was already blaming the victim for the bullies' actions.

"I want names," Alison said sternly. "I know those men from last night are behind this, and I know they're friends of yours."

"I can give you two of them." I didn't feel like I owed Sebastian and Louis any loyalty. They hadn't had any for me when they chose to trash the place where I worked, probably costing me my job in the process. "The others I don't really know that well."

"Two is a start, I suppose." She thrust a notepad and pen into my hands. "Write the names down. Addresses too, if you know where they live. Don't even think about lying to me, Rufus. If I find out you had any part in this, you'll be out that door so fast your feet won't touch the ground."

"I didn't, I swear." I handed the notepad back to her. I wanted so badly to ask about working in the kitchen and getting some time off at the weekend, but even someone as self-absorbed as me could tell it wasn't a good time. "I'll go and help Stuart and Jamie. Hopefully, we can get it all off before Landon sees it."

"Landon has already seen it," Alison replied, her no-nonsense tone even sharper than usual. "He'll be taking some time off, so you'll need to cover some of his tables."

Okay, so definitely not the right time to ask for a night

off. I got the distinct feeling I was being blamed not only for the vandalism outside, but for the fact we were going to be short-handed because of it. Nobody seemed willing to believe I'd had nothing to do with it.

I joined the others outside and between us we got the front windows clean with a few minutes to spare before the restaurant opened. Business was fairly quiet, which gave Alison another reason to stomp around with a face like thunder, but was something of a relief to Stuart, Jamie and I who had Landon's tables to wait on as well as our own.

Once we'd closed up for the night and Stuart and Jamie left, I went back to the office to find Alison. She sat at her desk, totting up the night's meagre takings.

"What do you want, Rufus?" she snapped without looking up. "I'm rather busy here."

"I know, sorry. I just wanted to ask if I can have Saturday night off."

"Oh, Rufus, really?" She turned to look at me in exasperation. "I told you Landon is on extended leave. I can't afford to be without you too."

"But, I promised my parents..."

"I said no, Rufus. Now, was there anything else?"

"Actually, yes." If she said no to a night off, I could only imagine what her reaction would be to my second request. I ploughed ahead anyway. "I'd like Landon's address, please."

"Absolutely not!" That was it. She didn't even ask why I wanted it. "Honestly, Rufus, what are you thinking? Do you have any idea how strict Landon's parents are? The trouble he'd be in if someone like you turned up on the doorstep?"

"Someone like me?" I echoed.

"Yes, someone like you. You're not exactly subtle about what you are."

"Landon's gay too. He told me."

"Maybe he is, but I doubt very much his parents are aware of that." Alison fixed me with a cold stare. "Stay away from him, Rufus. You've done enough."

"Okay, sorry. I just..." I had to stop speaking, the words stuck behind the sudden lump that had lodged in my throat. My eyes welled with tears; real ones too, not the fake-ass kind I usually forced to the surface when I was trying to get my own way over something. I dabbed at my wet eyes angrily, determined not to cry in front of Alison.

"Are you okay, Rufus? Are you ill?"

"No!" Why was that the first thing everyone, including my own mother, assumed? I was trying to be genuine, perhaps for the first time in my life, and everyone thought something had to be wrong with me. "I just... I want to see my mum."

Alison stared at me for an uncomfortably long moment. She didn't trust me, that much was obvious. I could practically hear the cogs turning in her brain as she tried to figured out if I was playing her or not. Her expression softened slightly and she sighed.

"Fine, you can have Saturday off. We'll manage somehow. You have to promise me, though, that you'll stay away from Landon."

"I promise," I said quickly. "Thank you."

I got out of there in a hurry and before she had a chance to change her mind.

"Hey, gayboy, You want a lift?"

Stuart sat in a car on the other side of the street from the restaurant. He had three other guys with him so I shook my head. Call me overly cautious, but I didn't trust straight guys much, especially when there were more than one of them in the same place at the same time. I had good reason not to. I knew from bitter experience that straight guys didn't appreciate little queers like me coming along and threatening their own sense of sexuality. I might not be as girlie-looking as Stefan, but I was feminine enough for some straight guys to fancy me without being sure why. Inevitably, it ended up being my fault.

"It's okay," I said. "It's not far. I can walk."

"Nah, come on. I gave fatso a lift last week. I can give you one too."

"You gave Landon a lift home?" That was unexpected, but it could be good news for me. After all, it wasn't as though I actually meant it when I promised Alison I'd stay away. "So, you know where he lives?"

"Yeah, one of those big fancy houses on Eastern Avenue. Why?"

"Never mind," I said, shrugging like it was no big deal. "See you tomorrow, Stuart."

CHAPTER 4

I STOOD at the end of the driveway and stared in awe at what had to one of the swankiest houses I'd ever set eyes on. I mean, the place was fucking huge, easily the biggest house on the street. It hadn't been hard to find. Eastern Avenue was one of those ultra-exclusive roads with only half a dozen enormous houses. I'd come here not knowing which house was Landon's, but the Porsche Boxster convertible in the driveway with Holby on the number plate was a big clue.

Well, I couldn't stand there all day just looking. That sort of behaviour was likely to get a man arrested in this neighbourhood. Some do-gooder neighbour would probably call the cops and accuse me of casing the joint of I hung around for too long.

Determined, I strode up the driveway and rang the doorbell. Even the chimes were fancy. I didn't know the name of the tune, but I recognised it as an old hymn. Alison's warning about Landon having strict parents who wouldn't approve of me suddenly made sense. It had been a mistake to come here. I'd meant to apologise to Landon, not make his life more difficult. It was too late to run away though. I could see the shadowy figure of a woman approaching through the frosted glass.

"Yes? Can I help you?"

The way she looked down her pointy nose at me, I half expected her to tell me to use the tradesman's entrance around the back. She looked nothing like Landon. Where he was... well, *round*... she was more like a walking, talking stick figure. Even her hair and eye colouring were totally different. I had a sudden moment of doubt. What if this wasn't Landon's mother at all, but a housekeeper or something? The family were obviously well off, but did they have servants? Did anyone have them these days?

"I'm... um...Rufus," I said, suddenly realising the woman, whoever she was, was still waiting for an answer. "I work with Landon. At the restaurant."

Yeah, like I needed to add that. I'm sure she didn't need telling where her own son worked. Assuming she was his mother, of course.

"Landon isn't working there currently," she replied haughtily. "So, what is it you want exactly?"

"I was just... well..." Shit. What did I want? I really should have thought this through instead of dashing over here on a whim.

"It's okay, Mum." Landon appeared in the doorway behind the woman. "I'll talk to him."

"Darling, please, how many times do I have to tell you?" Mrs. Holby's face tightened in displeasure. "Mum sounds so common. It's Mummy or Mother."

She shot me a withering look before turning and walking away along a wide, tiled hallway. Landon's bulk filled the doorway, his expression no friendlier than his stuck-up mother's.

"Did Alison send you with a message?" he asked. I noticed he didn't invite me inside. Probably worried I'd dirty up that squeaky-clean floor. "Let me guess. She changed her mind about giving me some time off."

"No, it's not that. In fact, she's given me Saturday off too."

Landon gave me a blank stare. "And you're telling me this because...?"

"I'm going to see my parents," I said, my mouth running way ahead of my brain. "You should come with me. To my parents. As a friend. Not like a date or anything."

"You're serious?" Landon blinked at me, totally dumbfounded. "Rufus, why on Earth would I want to go anywhere with you, let alone to visit your parents?"

Well, I guess I deserved that. I felt like a complete idiot and, the thing was, I didn't know what possessed me to ask him in the first place. We weren't friends. We hardly even knew each other. Put things right, I'd said, not turn up at his house acting like a deranged stalker. I wasn't the type of person who was easily embarrassed, but I could feel my face growing hot under Landon's intense gaze.

"Forget it," I muttered. "It was a stupid idea anyway." I backed away awkwardly, wondering if there was any way I could extract myself from the situation without looking like a complete and utter moron. "I... um... I should go."

"Yes." Landon was quick to agree. "You probably should."

He stepped back inside and shut the door, not slamming it in my face exactly, but close enough to it to send a clear message. *Get lost, Rufus.*

Before I could turn to leave, I heard the sound of raised voices on the other side of the door. Or rather, one raised voice, loud, shrill and angry. Landon's mother was tearing him a new one for allowing someone like me to tarnish her doorstep. What would the neighbours say? What would his father say when he got home? Landon wouldn't be returning to work at the restaurant, she said, not if it meant associating with sexual deviants and perverts like the abomination that had dared to show up at her house. I heard every word through the door. Maybe I shouldn't have stayed to listen, I didn't even mean to really, but somehow my feet refused to move.

The door flew open and Landon stormed out. He stopped abruptly when he saw me still standing there.

"Sorry," I said, slightly mortified that I'd been caught eavesdropping. "I was just..."

"Where do your parents live?"

"What?"

"Your parents?"

"Oh, right." I gawped at him, confused. "Sorry, what about them?"

"Where. Do. They. Live?" Landon said with painstaking slowness. "I'll come with you."

"You will?" I couldn't hide my surprise.

"I'm sick of them telling me what to do, so... yes. I'm doing it. I'm coming with you whether they like it or not."

CHAPTER 5

EARLY ON SATURDAY MORNING, I found myself waiting in a taxi at the end of Landon's driveway. I hadn't spoken to him since the other day, when he had agreed to come with me just to piss off his snooty mare of a mother. To be honest, I didn't expect him to show. He'd been angry when he'd said he'd come, lashing out to get back at his mother. Once he calmed down, he was bound to have had second thoughts. Maybe his parents would have talked him out of it. I didn't know either of them, but I was sure they would have tried. Landon was a grown man, but I got the impression his parents were still pretty controlling. No way would they condone their precious son going anywhere with – what had his mother called me? – a sexual deviant and an abomination.

The front door opened and Landon spilled out, an overnight bag slung over one shoulder. I saw the driver raise an eyebrow as Landon waddled over to the car. He caught my eye in the rear-view mirror and I scowled at him. It annoyed me that he was judging Landon on his appearance.

Probably, he judged me too for being short and slim and very obviously gay.

Don't forget hypocrite, a small voice said in the back of my head. I had a whole lifetime of experience in looking down my nose at people who didn't manage to live up to my exacting standards. It wasn't that long ago that I hadn't been able to see past Landon's layers of fat either. I didn't know when I'd gotten so protective of him, and I sure as Hell didn't know why. He wasn't my type, I reiterated to myself. I'd be a laughing stock among my friends if I was seen in public with someone like him. I mean, okay, his family was rich, but it was his parents' money not Landon's. There wouldn't be anything in it for me even if I did get with him. Which I wouldn't. Like I said – so not my type.

He climbed into the back seat me and flashed a shy smile. Even though I'd asked him to come with me, I hoped he didn't have the wrong idea about what was happening. I didn't want him thinking there was anything more to this than friends.

"Everything okay?" I asked.

There was still time for him to change his mind, and part of me hoped he would. It would save me a lot of embarrassment at being seen with him, and a lot of questions I'd rather not have to answer when we got to my parents. I'd told Mum I might be bringing a friend, which she automatically took to mean a boyfriend., and all my protests to the contrary had fallen on wilfully deaf ears. She was already overdosing on excitement at the thought of meeting the new man in my life. What she'd be expecting though, was someone who looked like me or Eric or Stefan. Someone small and somewhat on the feminine side. She'd have a shock when someone the size of a fucking elephant waddled up the garden path.

"Not really," Landon answered in that soft unassuming way he had about him. "I think I've probably been disinherited, and I'll have to go to confession every day for the next month before my parents will speak to me again.

"I didn't realise you were Catholic."

"I'm not, but that won't stop them," he muttered bitterly.

We were silent for the remainder of the short journey to the train station. It was kind of weird walking through the concourse to our platform. I was used to people staring at me, but most of the time I got those looks because of the way I dressed and my obvious love for all things purple. I'd toned down my appearance for the visit to my parents, but it wasn't me people were looking at anyway. It was Landon. It was hard to ignore the way people looked him up and down with the disgust or disdain they felt written clearly all over their faces. There were some, mainly the younger ones, who laughed openly at him or made derogatory comments as we passed. If I noticed, Landon had to have done, but he didn't say anything.

The train journey was excruciatingly uncomfortable. Landon seemed to withdraw more and more into himself the further we went, and for my part, I struggled to think of a single think to talk about. I passed the time by fiddling with my phone, while Landon stared morosely out of the window. Several times I glanced up and caught him watching me. Every time he quickly turned his head away, but not before I saw the wistful look on his face. I really hoped the fat lump wasn't falling for me, because that was the last thing I bloody needed.

From the station, we got a bus that conveniently deposited us at the end of my parents' road. Landon dragged his feet, trailing behind me. I forced down a knot of irritation. It was my own stupid fault. What had I been thinking, asking him to come with me in the first place?

"Keep up, can't you?" I snapped. It came out a little sharper than I'd intended, and I felt a twinge of guilt when Landon flinched. "We're almost there."

"What if they don't like me?"

"Of course they will." I ran a hand through my hair in exasperation. "Why wouldn't they?"

"My own parents don't like me that much," Landon said dryly. "Why should yours?"

I stopped walking and spun around to face him, frustration quickly turning to annoyance.

"Will you stop with the pity-party? I know what it's like not to be liked. I'm not exactly popular myself. You just need to man up and get over it. Show people you don't give a fuck, the same as I do."

"You?" Landon shot me a disbelieving look. "But you're perfect."

I laughed at that, even though I suppose it made sense that someone like him would look at someone like me and see perfection. Maybe he was a little bit jealous because I was everything that he wasn't.

"I'm not perfect. Far from it. When I was a kid, I was so ordinary it was painful. So, I changed myself. The clothes, hair, make-up..." I waved a hand up and down my body, although nothing about my appearance was particularly outlandish right at that moment. "It's like wearing a disguise. I'm not a nice person, Landon, so don't go thinking my asking you here means anything, because it doesn't. I've cheated on every boyfriend I've had, and trust me, there's been a lot of them."

"You're nice to me," Landon argued.

"Yeah, but I don't mean it. Not really."

Landon stared at me, his pudgy face filled with confusion.

"Then why did you ask me to come with you.?"

"I don't know." I shrugged. That much was true, at least. "I felt sorry for you, I suppose. Anyway, I didn't think you'd say yes. And even when you did, I didn't think you'd go through with it. In fact, I hoped you wouldn't."

"So why come and pick me up?" he countered. "You could have just come without me."

Okay, good point. He kind of had me there, because it was true. I could easily have told the taxi driver to go straight to the station, and not bothered going to Landon's house at all. So why had I, when I knew there was nothing in it for me?

"Why drag me here if you don't want me to stay?" Landon continued. "What am I supposed to do now? I don't have any money for a hotel. Are there even any around here?"

"A couple in town, yeah, but you don't have to do that. You can stay, Landon, just don't go thinking it makes us boyfriends or anything. Okay?"

"After you cheated on every guy you've ever been with?" Landon raised his eyebrows, fixing me with an incredulous look. "No offence, Rufus, but in the eventuality I one day get a boyfriend, I seriously hope I can do better than you."

Ouch. That hurt, but then I guess I asked for it. After all, I *had* told him I wasn't exactly the faithful type, whereas Landon probably wanted hearts and flowers and an eternal soulmate kind of relationship. Whatever. It wasn't as though I was interested in him anyway,

My mother was waiting on the doorstep when we walked up the garden path. She'd been the same since I was a little kid, known when I was going to appear, like she had some sort of freaky sixth sense. Of course, chances were, she'd known what time my train got in and therefore which bus I'd been on, but then that theory wasn't nearly as much fun as believing my mother was psychic.

She held out her arms and I stepped into her welcoming embrace without hesitation. It was always the same when I came home. One hug from my mum and I had to wonder why I stayed away for as long as I did. In her eyes, I wasn't the hard-faced, uncaring Rufus everyone knew and hated. I was just her son; plain old Rufus Bartholmew Haynes.

Once she was finally done hugging me, she held me at arms' length to inspect me from head to toe, another thing she habitually did whenever I arrived home.

"You're too thin," she tutted. "But you look taller. Have you grown, Rufie?"

"I'm twenty-six, Mum," I said, feeling the heat flood my face at the use of her pet name for me in front of Landon. "I don't think I'm going to grow anymore." I pulled away from her and jerked my head towards Landon. "This is my friend, by the way, Landon."

"Oh, well... hello, Landon." Her eyes widened slightly as she took in his appearance, and I really, *really* hoped she wasn't about to say anything to embarrass me. "You're a big lad, aren't you? I must say, you're not Rufie's usual type."

"We work together, Mum," I said, suddenly irritated. I pushed my way past her and into the house. "He's not my boyfriend."

I found Dad in the living room, sat in his armchair in front of the television, can of beer in hand while he watched a football match. I couldn't tell who was playing and, frankly, I didn't care. My lack of knowledge or interest in any sport whatsoever had always been a source of great disappointment to my dad, I knew that. He was fine with the whole being gay thing – or at least he said he was. It was the not liking football that he considered to be unforgiveable.

"Good journey?" he asked without looking away from the screen.

"Yeah, fine."

"Tom, this is Rufie's new friend, Landon," my mother said, with emphasis on the word 'friend' that implied she didn't entirely believe that was all Landon was.

"A pleasure to meet you, sir." Landon stepped forward and politely offered his hand for my father to shake.

I rolled my eyes. Well, of course he'd have impeccable manners. Putting me to shame in front of my parents was a bit much though.

Dad looked up at Landon in surprise, before taking his hand. I saw the way his eyes raked over Landon's massively obese figure. Then he got a pained expression on his face, like he didn't know what he should say next.

"Well, I suppose they say opposites attract," he muttered eventually.

"He is *not* my boyfriend!" I snapped crossly. "And, yes, he's really fat. Just get over it, for fuck's sake."

"Language, Rufus," my parents spouted simultaneously.

"And don't be so rude," Mum added. "I'm sure Landon can't help being overweight. What is it, sweetheart?" She smiled at Landon. "A thyroid problem?"

"Um... yes... something like that."

Or not, I thought, because he'd already told me he got to be that size by deliberately over-eating. Either he had lied to me then or he was lying to my mother now. I narrowed my eyes at him and he dropped his gaze to the floor, blushing. Mum was oblivious, totally charmed by Landon.

"Come with me to the kitchen, sweetheart," she said warmly, taking hold of Landon's arm. "You must be hungry after your long journey. We'll leave the boys to chat."

Uh oh. That didn't sound so good. My father and I hardly ever had full-on conversations. I'd had the same journey as Landon. How come I wasn't being fed? It wasn't as though we'd come that far anyway. London was only a couple of hours away, for fuck's sake.

"You worried your mother," Dad said once we were alone in the room. His eyes were back on the television, apparently finding watching the game more important than actually giving his only son his full attention. "What were you thinking, phoning late at night like that?"

"I don't know. I just wanted to talk to Mum, I guess."

"What's going on with you, Rufus?"

"Nothing. I told her not to worry."

"Yeah, right," Dad scoffed. "You say nothing's wrong and then you show up here with a guy who's so obviously not your type."

"You don't know my type," I argued, even though I was pretty sure he did. Every boyfriend I'd had was a skinny, little pretty boy just like me.

"I know enough to know that, normally, you wouldn't be seen dead with a guy like that ten-tonne-Tessie you're with. Is he rich? Is that it?"

"Dad!" I exclaimed, although I didn't know if I was objecting to what he'd called Landon or the assumption that my only interest in a man stemmed from the amount of money he had. "Is that really what you think of me?"

"Your mother doesn't want to see it, but I do," Dad continued. "I know you took that boy, Eric, for every penny he had and then threw him out when he lost his job."

"Uh... for the record... Eric left me for somebody else."

Which he had, although, admittedly, it was only after I'd thrown him out. Now, Eric was rolling in money and shacked up with a famous rock-star, while I had nothing. No money, no car and no home to call my home. All I had was a shitty job that didn't pay enough to keep me in the lifestyle to which I'd like to become accustomed. Even Stefan and Alex-bloody-Gill had their nice apartment and jobs they liked and were sorting their lives out in ways I could never seem to manage.

"What about those people you're staying with now?" Dad persisted. He always called Marcie and Killigan that. Those people. I suppose he and Mum had never really gotten over the fact that after I'd been held at gunpoint – a fake gun admittedly, but I hadn't known that at the time – I'd chosen to stay with Marcie and Killigan rather than come home to my parents. "Are you paying them rent, or are you sponging off them now?"

"I pay them rent," I said defensively.

Okay, it had only been recently, since I'd been working, and it wasn't much on the grand scale of things. Killigan would happily have taken more, but Marcie wouldn't hear of it. She told me I should be saving my money for when I was back on my feet and wanted to move into my own place again. Not that I was saving, of course. Money and I had only ever had a fleeting acquaintance, like ships that passed in the night.

I stood up, already regretting my decision to visit my parents. Regretting bringing Landon with me, whose appearance seemed to be the trigger for my father's latest round of disapproval. Regretting, most of all, that I was such a total fuck up and my life was going nowhere.

"I'll go and see what Mum and Landon are up to," I

said. Any excuse to escape the damn room and get away from his blatant disappointment in the way I turned out.

"Hmm," Dad mumbled vaguely, his eyes still glued to the television. "Make me a cup of tea while you're up, son."

I trudged, heavy footed, along the hallway. Maybe I was an arsehole because my dad was one. Like father like son. Wasn't that how the saying went? To be fair though, I knew that wasn't strictly true. Dad was an okay guy most of the time. I was the problem. The disappointment. The failure.

Mum and Landon were in the kitchen, standing side by side at the faux-marble counter top. She buttered bread and slid them across to Landon who cheerfully slapped slices of ham and cheese on top and closed them up to make sandwiches. They were chatting while they worked and Landon looked... happy. Happy and relaxed.

Jealousy washed over me. This was my home. These were my parents. This visit home was supposed to be about me, not him. Landon was hijacking everything and it wasn't fair. Maybe I should have kicked his fat arse to the kerb after all.

Striding across the kitchen, I snatched up one of the sandwiches and bit into it. I pulled a face, just to let him know his efforts didn't meet my exacting standards.

"Dad's in a mood," I mumbled around a mouthful of food.

"He worries about you," Mum said, flashing me a disapproving look. "As do I. Honestly, you're almost thirty, Rufus, and –"

"I'm twenty-six!"

"Close enough. What are you doing with your life, Rufus? You've got no job, no home, no boyfriend. No goals, that we can see. Is it any wonder we worry about you?"

"I have a job!" I protested. "And it's not like I'm living

on the streets, is it? As for goals, well, finding a rich boyfriend would be good. Preferably some really old guy who would die and leave me all his money, so I didn't have to fuck his wrinkly old arse."

"Oh, Rufus..." My mother rolled her eyes, but she didn't take the bait.

And, yeah, I knew I was being a dick, but I didn't seem capable of stopping myself. Everything was going wrong. Coming home was supposed to be another step on my path to self-improvement. Only the new me had fallen at the first hurdle and I wasn't sure if I should take it as some sort of omen. Maybe I wasn't meant to change who I was.

"I'll take our bags upstairs," I said, grudgingly. In a way, it was like giving myself a timeout for bad behaviour. Obviously, Landon and my mum were getting along just fine without me and I didn't really feel up to another dose of Dad's stoic disapproval, so hiding out in my old room for a while seemed to be my only option. "Landon's in the spare room, yeah?"

"Actually, sweetheart, you both are."

"What? Why?"

"Now, Rufus, be reasonable," Mum said, eyeing me warily, as though she fully expected to kick off at whatever she was about to tell me. "You're hardly ever here, so your father decided to turn your old room into a man-cave. It's really very nice. You should –"

"Hold on a minute." I cut her off abruptly. "Why my room? If he wanted a stupid man-cave, why not turn the spare room into one?"

"Because we need the spare room for when people come to stay." My mother looked at me, as though the answer should be perfectly obvious. "And the spare room has a double bed, so you and Landon will be just fine in there."

"I am *not* sharing a bed with Landon!"

Turning on my heel, I stormed out, slamming the door so hard behind me it rattled the windows in their frames. I didn't know where I was going and I didn't care. Everything was messed up. I was supposed to be their little boy and maybe I didn't come home as often as I should, but to take my fucking room away? That was harsh. All that 'needing the room for visitors' bullshit was just that. Bullshit. I was an only child. Both my parents were only children too, so there no aunts, uncles or cousins. My grandparents on both sides were long gone, so who were all these fucking people who supposedly came to stay all the time?

"Rufus."

"Huffing out a frustrated sigh, I closed my eyes and counted to ten before turning to face Landon. I should have known the big lump would follow me. If he had been the one to stomp out, I wouldn't have followed him, but Landon was better than that. He was better than me full stop.

"I'm sorry," he said.

"Why are you sorry? You're not the one who turned my bedroom into a stupid fucking man-cave."

"No, I know, but... I don't think they did it to hurt you."

"Yeah? Well, guess what? They did."

God, I was such a child. Having a tantrum in the street because my parents had taken away a room I didn't really want in the first place.

"I don't blame you for not wanting to sleep with me," Landon said awkwardly, his pudgy face instantly flooding with colour. "I don't mean *sleep* with me. I mean go to bed with me. No, wait! Share a bed. I mean share a bed. I sweat," he babbled. "I sweat a lot. Nobody in their right mind would want to be in the same bed."

"Relax, big fella," I said, surprising myself as much as Landon when I laughed. "It's for one night. I'm sure I'll survive."

"You don't have to," Landon mumbled.

"It's fine," I told him as we headed back towards the house. "But I swear to God, if I drown in your sweat during the night, I'll come back and haunt you."

"Deal," Landon said, and I glanced up to see the faintest glimmer of a smile on his face.

CHAPTER 6

BY SOME MIRACLE, I did survive a night in the same bed as Landon, although it was a bit of a close-run thing. He'd been telling the truth about the sweating though. Even with the window open, there was an unpleasant stale odour in the room, and the sheet felt distinctly damp. He snored too, loudly, keeping me awake for most of the night. Like I said, I survived. I didn't say anything about enjoying the experience.

Landon was hugely apologetic in the morning and jumped straight into the shower as soon as he got out of bed. Strangely, the whole episode didn't annoy me as much as I would have thought it would. Given his size, he probably couldn't help sweating, and I imagined the same went for the snoring. Okay, so maybe being a fat bastard *was* his fault, but who was I to judge?

Yes, I was on another "be-a-better-person" kick. Funny how it all seemed to begin and end with Landon. I totally didn't get it. It wasn't like I fancied him or anything. I couldn't repeat that little fact often enough. I wouldn't get anything out of it, so what was the point?

The second day spent with Mum and Dad was hugely more successful than the first. They treated us to Sunday lunch at a pub less than ten minutes' drive from the house. Apparently, it was their favourite place and they regularly went there for dinner, which I hadn't known. There seemed to be a lot they didn't tell me about their everyday lives and, at first, it rankled a little bit, until my newfound conscience reminded me that I didn't exactly share much with them either. So – as with Landon's snoring – I pushed away the small niggle of annoyance and ignored it.

I had to do it again while I watched my parents interact with Landon far more naturally than they ever did with me. They obviously liked him and he seemed to feel the same way about them. It crossed my mind that maybe they would have preferred someone like Landon for a son, fat and all. Then again, if he'd grown up with my mum and dad instead of his own, he wouldn't have found it necessary to eat his way into obesity to hide who he really was. I leaned back in my chair and watched as they all laughed over something Dad said, and shit... I didn't know the man even had a sense of humour. I appeased my wounded pride by telling myself there was probably a family out there who would see *me* as their perfect son. Probably families whose own offspring had turned out to be mass murderers or something. That was the only way anyone would consider me to be an improvement.

Truth was, I found I didn't altogether mind that Mum and Dad had taken to Landon like they had. He was relaxed and smiling and, for once, he wasn't thinking about his weight and what other people thought of him. He talked more during the course of that meal than he had in the entire time I'd known him. It warmed my cold, black heart to see him happy. Landon happy made me happy, I realised. Annnnd... okay, I needed to shut that shit down right there.

Jesus, what was the fucking guy doing to me, making me go all soppy and gooey-eyed every time I looked at him? Like I was the fucking Grinch and my heart grew a whole two sizes larger every time he smiled. I didn't like him that way. I didn't. He wasn't hot or sexy, and he certainly didn't have a body I could see myself lusting after. So why did he seem to reach that small distant part of me that nobody else ever had? Not even Eric, and I'd loved him. In my own way, of course.

"Are you okay there, son? You're very quiet."

"Huh?" I gave my father a dazed look, suddenly realising he was speaking to me.

"I said, you're very quiet."

All three of them stared in my direction, eyes clouded with suspicion. They probably thought I was secretly devising some sort of dastardly revenge plan to punish them for ignoring me.

"I'm fine." I pushed away my empty plate and gave them a weak grin. "Just enjoying my lunch."

I wasn't fooling anybody, but they seemed relieved to know I wasn't about to cause a scene. Once Mum excused herself to go to the ladies' room and Dad went back to the bar for another round of drinks, Landon shuffled into the chair next to mine.

"Sorry," he said. "I'm monopolising all of your parents' time. They should be paying you attention. Not me. I shouldn't have come." He sighed heavily. "I'm such a selfish idiot. No wonder you hate me."

"I don't hate you, Landon. I don't know what's wrong with me lately. Things have got a bit confusing."

"Oh, okay." Landon looked at me doubtfully. I didn't

blame him. Our friendship – if that's even what this was – wasn't at the stage at confiding in each other yet. Plus, he'd been hurt enough times before that he was just waiting for me to turn on him. "You could... I mean if you want to... you can talk to me."

"Thanks, but right now I think this is something I have to figure out for myself."

How could I talk to him about my problem when I was pretty sure he *was* my problem? Him and his puppy dog eyes, messing with my head and making me feel things I wasn't used to feeling.

Later, as we were leaving, Dad put his arms around me and pulled me into an unexpected – and rare – hug. I couldn't remember the last time he'd hugged me, but it was probably when I was a kid. He certainly hadn't offered up any kind of physical comfort when he came to visit when I'd been hospital after being beaten up, or after I'd been held at gunpoint by Mason's crazy ex. Fake gun, yeah, I already said that, but it still hurt like fuck when the nutter hit me with it. So, for him to hug me was surprising, but not entirely unwelcome.

"You got yourself a good one, Rufus," Dad said quietly. "Don't mess it up this time."

"He's not my boyfriend, Dad."

"Well, then maybe he should be. Don't let him go, Rufus. You like him. I can tell."

I pulled away from him with a little shake of my head. Maybe there was some small part of me that liked Landon, but it was only as a friend. We could never be anything else, especially when he wasn't even out to his family. Shit, I wasn't even that sure he was out to himself yet, given that he chose to bury his sexuality beneath a mountain of blubber rather than accept it as a part of who he was.

CHAPTER 7

AFTER DROPPING Landon off at his house on the way home from the station, I didn't see him again for a couple of days. Marcie welcomed me back with open arms and an endless supply of hot chocolate with whipped cream on top. Killigan pointed out in a sour tone that I'd only been gone for one night and she couldn't possibly have had time to miss me. He followed it up with a wink though, so I took it to be an attempt at teasing me. For once, he didn't give me a hard time and I was glad, because although seeing my parents had been nice, this house and the people in it were my home now.

Monday and Tuesday both Marcie and Killigan had to work, so I looked up recipes on the internet and did my best to cook a nice evening meal for them. I even bought the ingredients with my own money, which Marcie said I didn't have to while Killigan seemed quietly impressed and actually called me 'son' like he did with Stefan and Alex. And, yes, my heart swelled just a little bit to hear that little word fall from the big man's lips. I was sure Landon would say pride was a sin, but I couldn't help it; and by the time

Killigan had all but licked his plate clean and finished heaping praise onto my culinary efforts, it was a wonder I could fit my big head through the doorway.

Wednesday evening, I reluctantly trudged my way to the restaurant for my first shift of the week. I still harboured hopes of eventually being allowed to move into the kitchen, but I had to accept it was something that wasn't going to happen overnight. I guess I had to prove to Alison that I wouldn't let her down if she gave me a chance, and the best way of doing that was by first of all stepping up my game as a waiter. I'd be charming and helpful for maybe the next month or so and then I'd politely remind her of my desire to become a chef.

The funny thing was, I'd learned something over the weekend with Landon and my parents, and the couple of days that followed with Marcie and Killigan. All this time, I'd been so focused on getting – by whatever means necessary – the material things that I wanted, that I'd neglected the things that actually made me happy. I'd discovered that I liked being liked. For so long, I'd never even really liked myself, because I knew what sort of horrible person I was. But now, my father's hug, Landon's shy smile, Marcie and Killigan's pleasure in the food that I cooked for them – those simple things filled me with more warmth that a faux fur jacket ever could. It was as though I'd had my very own Ebenezer Scrooge style epiphany, except it wasn't Christmas and I doubted that I was thoroughly reformed, however much I wanted to be.

Landon showed up for his shift to, which surprised me; especially as his stuck-up mother had tried to dictate that he couldn't work at the restaurant anymore if it meant associating with the likes of me. Perhaps I wasn't the only one whom life had given a wake-up call, and Landon was experiencing an epiphany of his own. I hoped so, because he was a decent guy. He deserved to be happy far more than I did.

His logic was, if his parents still weren't talking to him, then they couldn't tell him that he wasn't allowed to go to work.

Understandably, Alison had concerns about his early return to work and for a moment it looked as though she might send him home again. I finished tying my apron and went to stand in the open doorway to her office.

"Don't worry. I'll keep an eye on him."

"You?" Alison looked at me doubtfully. "Why would you look out for him?"

"Because that's what friends do for each other, isn't it?" I winked at Landon and was rewarded by his anxious frown becoming a small smile. Only a very small one, but it was better than nothing.

"Friends?" Alison echoed, her gaze flashing between the two of us in disbelief. "Rufus, I don't know what game you're playing, but..."

"No games," I promised, crossing my heart with my forefinger like a little kid. "So, can he stay?"

"Fine," she said, still not totally convinced. "But only because Jamie phoned in sick and I need him."

Landon hurried off to change into his uniform before she could change her mind. I hesitated in the doorway, wanting to say something about learning to cook, but in the end, I kept my mouth shut. It was too soon. She didn't trust me yet, and I couldn't blame her really, because she still thought she was dealing with the Rufus of old. I had to show her I'd changed. Or at least I was trying to.

"So, are you two bum chums now then?" Stuart asked when I joined him and Landon out on the restaurant floor.

"Who sticks it to who? Wait, can fat-boy even find his dick in all that blubber? I bet he hasn't seen it for years."

Landon turned away, his face bright red. I rounded on Stuart with a sudden surge of anger. Why did straight guys think it was okay to ask that? Not that me and Landon were fucking, but even so, it was none of Stuart's damn business. I didn't go around asking every straight guy I met if their girlfriends ever strapped on a dildo and ploughed their arses, did I? No, and that was because it was none of my business what they did in the bedroom, and I didn't care anyway.

"You know what? I might be smaller than you..." I was by about four inches. "... but next time you make a comment like that, this little faggot is going to wipe the fucking floor with you. Do you get that, you homophobic arsehole?"

Stuart laughed, not threatened by me in the slightest. Okay, that dented my pride a bit, but whatever.

"You and whose army, short-stuff?" he asked mockingly.

"How about this army?"

We all spun around, Stuart flushing guiltily, as we realised Alison had come into the restaurant and heard the entire exchange.

"We were just messing around, weren't we, guys?" Stuart blustered. "Bit of banter before we open. Right, Rupert?"

"It's Rufus, idiot," I said, folding my arms and glaring at him.

"Okay, try this for banter," Alison said, giving Stuart one of the coldest looks I'd ever seen. "Next time *I* hear you make a homophobic remark in my restaurant, *I* will wipe the fucking floor with you. No army required. Plus, you'll be out of a job. Now do you get it?"

"Yes, sorry," Stuart muttered, shame-faced. "Sorry, Rufus. Sorry... um... shit, I don't even know your name."

"It's Landon," I supplied helpfully, because Landon stood in a corner looking absolutely mortified, even though he hadn't really had any involvement with what had just happened.

"Well, don't stand around looking gormless. Get back to work, all of you. Rufus." Alison held out a set of keys. "Open the doors for me, please."

I took the keys from her, slight dumbfounded. Alison always opened up herself, never trusting any of us lesser mortals to carry out the unlocking of a door to her meticulous standards. Stupid as it sounds, my hands shook slightly as I turned the key in the lock. I had to stand on tiptoe to reach the bolt at the top of the door, but I managed it without mishap and proudly returned the keys to Alison.

She nodded, the closest I was going to get to a smile, I supposed. Then she turned and headed back to her office. The first customers were already coming through the door and they chose a table in Stuart's section. I looked over at Landon. He smiled and gave me a thumbs-up, knowing what it meant to me to have Alison's approval.

And didn't that mess with my head, because Landon got it. After spending only two days together, he got *me*; more than most people did who'd known me for months, or even years. What did that mean? Mum always said there was someone out there for everybody and I'd know when I met the man who was destined to be my soulmate. But that couldn't be what this was. My soulmate was supposed to be handsome, sexy and preferably rich. He wasn't supposed to be some bloated whale with nice eyes and a smile to die for...

Stop it! I wasn't falling for Landon, however nice he

was, or however suited to me he might turn out to be. I refused to let it happen. We worked together. I could be a friend if he wanted, but that was it. That was all it would ever be. I was taking a lot for granted anyway. Landon wasn't even out, and he'd made it quite clear that, even if he was, he could do a lot better than me when it came to boyfriends.

Being a Wednesday, the restaurant was fairly quiet, although we each had at least two tables of diners in our sections. Landon had four tables at one point and as my diners already had their meals, I gave him a hand bringing the food out.

Stuart gave us the stink-eye, but only when he knew Alison couldn't see him, and he didn't dare say anything. I didn't care what he thought anyway. For the first time ever, I enjoyed my shift. Landon seemed to be enjoying himself more than usual too, and – deep down – I liked to think it was because of me. Overall, the atmosphere in the restaurant felt friendlier and more relaxed than ever before. The customers picked up on it too, because they smiled and chatted while they ate, complimented the chef and left tips that were way more than generous than normal. Alison was delighted, which meant we didn't end the night getting chewed out by the boss for once.

I shared the tips out between me, Landon and Stuart, confused when Stuart tried to hand half of his back.

"I didn't earn it," he murmured. "It was you and Landon that created the good vibe in here tonight. Not me."

"You were here too, weren't you?"

"Yeah, but..."

"We're a team," Landon added. "So, we share the tips."

"Seriously? Thanks, guys."

Stuart took his money and left. Landon and I moved a

little slower. Not that we didn't want to go home; we weren't just in any great hurry. I was aware of Alison watching us from her office, while trying her best to look as though she wasn't. Last week, she had been warning me off, and now she was acting like she might actually approve of me and Landon being together. Not that we *were* together. We were friends. It was other people who seemed intent on making it something more.

"I'd better go," Landon said. "My dad is picking me up. It would probably be better if he didn't see us together."

"He doesn't know me, does he?"

"No, but Mum's told him all about you. The evil homo-sexual trying to corrupt their innocent son." He was teasing me, which was kind of cute in a way. I didn't know he had it in him. "They're still praying for my soul, but don't worry, I think I've convinced them that my virginity is still intact."

I arched an eyebrow. "You're a virgin? Really?"

"Night, Rufus," he said, smiling softly before he slipped out of the back door.

CHAPTER 8

"YOU'RE IN A GOOD MOOD," Killigan said, coming up behind me and reaching around to dip his finger into the pot I had on the stove.

"Hey!" I smacked the back of his hand with the wooden spoon I was holding. "That's very rude, you know?"

"Mmmm." He sucked the sauce from his fingers, totally unrepentant. "Tastes good, though. Have you talked to your boss about moving into the kitchen at work yet?"

"Yeah, last night."

It had been two weeks since Landon and I had returned from the trip to my parents and, so far, I had managed to keep up the charm offensive while at the restaurant. It seemed to be working too. Alison was always telling me how impressed she was with me and Golden Boy Jamie had slipped right down the ranks on her list of favourites. He was the only one who didn't seem to get that things had changed and was still struggling to get his head around the fact he couldn't get away with half the shit he used to. Stuart was quiet at times, but he seemed to understand that Landon and I were running the show now. He did his best to be friendly and work alongside us. If I thought I had changed, it was nothing compared to Landon. His confidence had increased tenfold, and he laughed and smiled more than I had even seen him do in the whole time I'd known him.

"What did she say?" Killigan asked, dragging me out of my daydream.

"Actually, she said I could do it, as soon as she finds a replacement for me waiting tables."

"That's good then, isn't it?" Killigan ignored my icy glare and stuck his finger in the chilli again. I hoped he would burn himself, but no such luck. The bastard apparently had asbestos fingertips. "Only you don't sound too sure."

"No, I am sure. It's definitely something I want to do, but... I don't know. I kind of like being a waiter at the moment too."

Killigan shot me a knowing look. "Because of this guy, Landon?"

"What? No!" I turned my back on him and concentrated on ferociously stirring the chilli. "Well, maybe a bit. We work well together, that's all. Once I go into the kitchen, I won't see as much of him."

Okay, that was more than I intended to admit out loud, but the sad fact was it was true. I enjoyed working alongside Landon. He was quite funny in his own shy, unassuming way and good company too. We usually found a few moments during our shift when we could just talk which was... nice. I'd never had that with anyone before. Not even with Eric. We'd loved, we'd fucked and we'd fought, but we'd seldom sat and had conversations about anything important. Maybe the difference was that I didn't actually want anything from Landon. I didn't want sex with him, or money to pay my bills. I didn't expect him to buy me stuff either. For probably the first time in my life, I liked being around someone just for the company they offered.

"Why don't you invite him to the wedding?"

I shrugged, my mood souring instantly. "What wedding?"

"Rufus, come on. I thought you and Alex were okay now?"

"Doesn't mean I want him marrying Stefan."

Saying we were 'okay' was stretching it a bit anyway. We tolerated each other long enough to team up and rescue Stefan from his abusive father, but it hadn't taken long before we were back to barely being able to be in the same room together without a whole lot of sniping on his part and bitching on mine. The fact the macho arsehole was marrying the love of my life was a joke. Privately, I still held onto the hope that Stefan would see the light and not go through with it. Better still, he'd dump Alex altogether and come back to where he belonged. Which was namely with me.

"You know, you're going to have to accept it sooner or later," Killigan said, shaking his head. "And sooner would be better seeing as they're getting married in three weeks' time."

"Don't remind me," I said, with an inelegant snort.

"All I'm saying," Killigan continued, "is that you might find it easier if you had someone there with you."

"Yeah, well, there's no point asking him anyway, because Alison isn't going to give us both the same weekend off again, is she?" I lifted the pan off the heat and changed the subject. "This is done. Do you want to call Marcie while I plate up?"

"Plate up," Killigan chuckled. "Listen to you, talking like a pro already."

I left them to their meal and went to get ready for work. Half an hour later, as I was walking down the road to the restaurant, I was still thinking about what Killigan had said. Not about accepting Stefan and Alex getting married soon, because if I was honest, I didn't think I'd ever fully accept that. And, okay, when it actually happened, I might have to *accept* it, but I was certain I was never going to be happy about it.

No, what was really on my mind was what he'd said about Landon. It might be nice to have him there, but what would he think if I invited him? Asking him to be my plus one for my best friend's wedding was sort of a big deal, because it would definitely be seen as a date this time, not just by Landon, but by everyone else too. People didn't take *friends* to weddings, did they? They took their partners, boyfriends, girlfriends, whichever way they swung, but not workmates, which was, essentially, all that Landon was.

I didn't mind being seen as Landon's friend, but I still didn't want people to assume we were together. Not that I had been there for a few weeks now, but I could just hear the conversations that would be take place at Keane's, the local gay club and home to the biggest bitchfest in the whole of London. *Have you seen what Rufus is with now? How fucking desperate has Rufus got these days, to be seen in public with that beached whale? Oh, my God, Rufus couldn't lower his standards anymore if he tried.* I knew exactly the way it would go, because usually I would be the one in the midst of those conversations; instigating them even, about other people.

Landon was in the staff changing room when I arrived. He looked up with a smile and my heart did that stupid little fluttering thing it did when I saw him. I shut that shit down fast, not wanting to even think about what it meant.

"Did Alison tell you?" I asked, my voice colder than was strictly necessary. It wasn't him I was mad at, but myself. Or maybe it was him, because he was the one with that big goofy face that melted my heart a little bit more every time I was close to him. "She's given me a job in the kitchen. I'm going to be a chef, so I won't be waiting tables anymore."

"Oh." Landon's smile faded and he looked at me, a little crestfallen. "Well, I'm pleased for you, Rufus. I know it's what you wanted."

"Thanks."

Although I didn't have the right to feel that way, I was slightly put out by his response. I didn't want him to be pleased for me. I wanted him to be at least a tiny bit upset that I was breaking up our happy team. My head was a fucking mess. I deliberately pushed him away and got my feelings hurt when he went. Then I'd reel him back him, only to get scared and reject him again when he got too close. If I didn't sort myself out soon, he'd give up on me altogether, and I wasn't sure what I would do if I lost him for good.

"So, are you in the kitchen from tonight?" Landon said lightly. He tied his apron and avoided my gaze, acting like he didn't care when obviously he did. It made me feel a little better, although I could never admit that to anyone but myself.

"Alison has to replace me first," I told him. "I'll probably start in a couple of weeks after I get back from Weymouth."

"Right. I forgot you're going away. A friend's wedding, isn't it?"

"Yeah," I said shortly, still preferring not to talk or even think about Stefan marrying that oversized dickhead.

"Well, I suppose we should show willing." Landon gestured to the doorway awkwardly and made to move around me so he could go out to the restaurant.

"Landon." He stopped. I opened my mouth. Closed it again. Opened it a second time. "Come with me."

"What do you mean? Where?"

"To Weymouth. Stefan's wedding."

"Rufus." Landon took a step back and stared at me, chewing his fleshy bottom lip doubtfully. "Is this going to be like when you asked me to go to your parents? Are you going to change your mind about wanting me there as soon as we arrive?"

"No, I... I just... Look, I don't even want to go myself, okay? I could do with a friend there. You don't have to if you don't want to. Forget I asked."

"No, I want to," Landon said quickly. Too quickly, in fact, and he blushed. "As a friend, of course. I know I'm not going as your boyfriend or anything."

"Whatever." I shrugged, refusing to allow myself to being the slightest bit pleased that he'd agreed to come. I didn't care either way. Really. I didn't.

CHAPTER 9

"THIS HAS to be the stupidest idea ever," I complained, for what had to be the thousandth time that day, and it wasn't even lunchtime.

"Sweetheart, you're the one who invited him," Marcie pointed out from the front seat.

"Yeah, well... I've changed my mind," I snapped back crossly.

Killigan made a deep grumbling noise and glared at me in the rear-view mirror, his not-so-subtle way of warning me not to take my bad mood out on Marcie. I'd been in a temper for days, ever since I found out Eric and Mason were flying in for Stefan's wedding. I mean, why the fuck would they? Okay, so Eric had stayed with Stefan and Alex for a short while after I'd kicked him out of our flat, but Stefan was my friend, not his. Alex didn't have any friends in the first place, so it wasn't like they were coming for him. Mason was meant to be touring America with his band as well, but somehow he'd managed to find time in his busy schedule to fly across the Atlantic to go to the wedding of two people he didn't even know.

"They're all going to think Landon's my boyfriend," I whined. "Eric's going to laugh his nuts off if he thinks Landon is the best I can do after him. And what about Stefan? What's he going to say when he sees me with that walking tub of lard?"

"Don't say that," Marcie scolded lightly. "And Stefan is your best friend. I'm sure he'll be over the moon that you have found someone as lovely as Landon."

I rolled my eyes at the back of Marcie's head. See, that right there was what I was on about. If she was going to go around talking like Landon was my boyfriend, then the others were bound to believe it. I hadn't *found* Landon. Stefan and Eric wouldn't be happy for me either. They'd think it was hilarious; that I'd got what I deserved after all my years of bed-hopping with strictly beautiful people.

"Can't you just drive past and not bother picking him up?" I said, remembering that's exactly what Landon had said I should do when I didn't want him at my parents' house.

"Too late. We're already here," Killigan said, pulling up at the end of Landon's driveway. He twisted round in his seat to face me. "This is Stefan and Alex's weekend, Rufus. Don't make it all about you."

I slumped back in my seat, sulking; scowling at Landon as he waddled up the driveway, like it was his fault I fucked up again. Actually, he didn't waddle as much as he used to. He'd lost some weight over the past few weeks. Not much, he was still huge, but I noticed even if nobody else did.

Killigan hopped out and put his bag in the boot of the car. Then they both got back in, with Landon joining me on the back seat. His face was flushed and angry, and he looked upset. It didn't take a genius to work out his stuck-up parents had probably given him a hard time for going away with me again. Still, it wasn't my problem. I nodded a curt greeting, but I didn't bother speaking to him. A hurt expression crossed his face and for a moment I thought he was going to cry.

"Is everything okay, sweetheart?" Marcie asked gently when it became clear I wasn't about to say anything.

"No, not really," Landon answered, his voice tight. "My parents said if I left the house this morning, I needn't bother going home."

He left the rest unspoken, but his meaning was clear. Basically, he just got kicked out of his home for agreeing to come on this little jolly with me and for what? For me to not speak to him? For me to make it clear I didn't want him to come? Again.

I felt kind of guilty, but if they'd given him an ultimatum and he'd chosen to leave, that was on him.

"You don't have to come," I offered lamely. "You could go back right now and tell them you changed your mind."

"I haven't changed my mind," Landon said, staring straight ahead. "Whatever happens, I want to spend this time with you, Rufus."

"Well, don't you worry about it," Marcie assured him. "If you need somewhere when we get back, you can come and stay with us."

"What?" Killigan and I exclaimed at the same time.

I couldn't believe she'd offer him a room like that without asking me, her existing lodger, or – perhaps more importantly – her live-in lover. Why was she so intent on pushing me and Landon together? I was quite capable of finding my own boyfriends, thank you very much, even if I hadn't exactly been looking since getting friendly with Landon. In my mind, that was one more reason for getting rid of the fat lump. Hanging around with him was seriously affecting my sex life.

"Don't worry about it now," Marcie said sweetly. "We don't want to spoil things for Alex and Stefan, do we? We can discuss it when we get home."

The journey was a tense and uncomfortable one. And, yes, I had to hold my hands up and admit it was entirely my fault. I stared out of one side window and refused to talk to anyone. Landon stared out of the other, awkward and miserable. Killigan drove in grim silence, while Marcie at least tried to keep a conversation going, but gave up after a few miles passed without getting a response from any of us.

When we reached Weymouth, Killigan surprised me by pulling up outside a hotel about five minutes' walk form the seafront.

"This is you, boys. We'll be back to pick you up later for dinner."

"What? Why are we staying here? I thought we were staying at Tony's."

"Killigan and I will be at Tony's," Marcie said. "Stefan is staying there tonight, and Eric and Mason too, so there's really not room for all of us."

"Hold on, why are Eric and Mason staying there? Mason can afford a hotel room. I can't."

"That's why you're not paying," Killigan answered gruffly. "I am. I booked it for you as soon as I knew Eric and Mason were coming over. They can't stay at a hotel because Mason doesn't want the media knowing he's over here and turning the wedding into a circus."

"And you didn't bother telling me before now?"

I jumped out of the car and grabbed my bag from the boot. I heard Landon thanking Killigan and rolled my eyes. What a fucking suck-up. He appeared beside me a few moments later and pulled out his own bag. He waved as Killigan and Marcie pulled away and I rolled my eyes again. Landon trudged behind me as I walked up to the front desk to find Killigan had only booked us one room. There was a sinking feeling in my gut as we climbed the stairs (what kind of hotel didn't have an elevator in this day and age, for fuck's sake?) and pushed open the door.

There was a double bed in the room. Of course there was. What else would it be?

"Fuck my life," I snarled at the world in general, throwing my bag onto the bed.

Landon sighed as he closed the door. "You promised you wouldn't do this, Rufus."

"Do what?" I fired back, though I knew exactly what he meant. I was on a downward spiral and old Rufus was back in charge with his old Rufus ways and behaviour. Inside, I felt so angry without even knowing why.

"You said you wouldn't ask me to go somewhere with you if you didn't mean it. You said you wouldn't get nasty again."

"I am *not* being nasty!"

"Yes, you are, Rufus, and it's not fair. You invited me here. I fell out with my parents and probably got kicked out of my house because of you, and now you won't even give me the time of day."

"You don't understand," I said, exasperated, because he had to have looked in a mirror at some point. He knew what he looked like and he had to know someone like me would never be with someone like him. Just as he had to know how it would look to everyone who saw us together; especially if they found out we were sleeping in the same bed. "My ex-boyfriend is here, Landon. He screwed me over for a super-rich, famous rock-star who happens to be as hot as fuck, and

I don't want him thinking you're the best I can do these days."

"Gee, thanks."

"You know what I mean. I don't want them laughing at me and thinking I'm reduced to scraping the bottom of the barrel since Eric left."

"You know what?" Landon snapped, suddenly developing a surprising amount of fire in that substantial belly of his. "You're no catch either, Rufus. You're better looking than me, I can't argue with that, but you're not a nice person. Maybe I'm the one who should be worried about what people think. Maybe I don't want people thinking I can't do any better than you. They'll see us together and they'll think the only reason you're with me is because I have money. Which I don't, by the way, but your friends don't know that and they're going to think I'm a pathetic loser for falling for it."

"Fuck you!" I yelled angrily. Because, seriously, who did he think he was to say that shit about me? He'd be lucky to have me and he knew it. Anyway, this wasn't about Landon. Who cared what people thought of him? It was about me, and my ex-boyfriend seeing me as a joke. Not to mention what Stefan would think. I'd have no chance of finally getting him away from Alex if he thought I had a fat boyfriend. "I need a drink. I assume this shithole has a bar."

Landon hesitated. "Do you want me to come with you?"

I shot him a withering look. "What do you think?"

CHAPTER 10

BY THE TIME Landon summoned the nerve to come looking for me, I was on my fourth gin. Maybe my fifth, but who was counting? I didn't even really like the stuff, but different flavoured gins were all the rage at the moment and, hey... I liked to keep up with the latest trends.

The bar was quiet, just me and a couple of business looking types and a bored guy serving the drinks. All three of them kept giving me funny looks.

I saw Landon as soon as he walked in, but then he was hard to miss with all that flab wobbling about. He ordered a diet coke – which made me roll my eyes, because what was the point? – and carried it over to my table in the corner.

"Can I join you?"

"Suit yourself." I shrugged, like I couldn't care less.

Secretly, I was pleased he'd come to find me; and just a little bit pissed off that it had taken him so long. He sat, and cleared his throat, working himself up to say something I probably wasn't going to want to hear.

"This place is a dump," I said quickly, jumping in before he had the chance.

"It's not so bad," Landon replied, glancing around. "Actually, we stayed here a few months ago for my sister's birthday."

"Bullshit." I raised my eyebrows at him, disbelieving. "You're telling me your snotty, extremely well-off parents stayed in this hotel?"

"Yes, well... I heard my father on the phone a while back. He said something about his business being in trouble or being in debt. I didn't catch the whole conversation, but that was the gist of it. Thing is, I don't think my mother knows. He lied to her when we came here. Told her he'd left it too late to book and everywhere else was full."

"And she believed it?" I scoffed. His mother had to be as stupid as she looked if she bought that particular line of crap.

"Of course she did. She's like the perfect Stepford Wife, remember?"

"She's a what?" I furrowed my brow at him, trying to make sense of it. The effect of the four (or five) gins I'd downed in quick succession suddenly hit me, and my brain was getting a little fuzzy.

"Never mind." He glanced around the room again. "Those guys keep staring at us."

"At me," I corrected. "It's probably the purple hair and eye shadow."

"And the purple jeans and boots," Landon added with a wry smile.

"So, I like purple." I'd dyed it especially for the wedding, despite my reservations going to the whole stupid farce at all. "Sue me."

"What would be the point? I know you haven't got any money."

"Ha ha. You're a funny guy."

"You know, I don't get you, Rufus," he said, turning serious again. "I thought we were friends, yet you blow hot and cold with me all the time. I don't understand why you ask me to go places with you and then act like you don't want me around."

"You mess with my head, Landon." It had to be the booze talking, because there was no way I'd tell him how I felt if I was sober. "I can't be with you. I just can't, because..."

"Because I'm fat and ugly?" Landon finished for me, his big brown eyes shimmering with sudden tears.

"No, that's not it. And you're not ugly. I told you before, you have really nice eyes, and you have a smile to die for."

"Rufus..." Landon said uncertainly.

"Thing is, you're right. You deserve better than me." I blundered on, my damn mouth running too fast for my fuzzy brain to keep up. "I'll only end up hurting you and I don't want to do that. Not this time. Not to you."

"Rufus," Landon said again, but softer this time, like he felt sorry for me.

His pity was the last thing I needed, because before I knew it, I was fucking crying too. Between the two of us, we were certainly putting on a show for the other people in the bar. What a sight we must make: the purple clad pretty boy in make-up and the beached whale, both sat there blubbing like babies.

"The only time I'm happy is when I'm with you," I babbled, letting the booze do the talking. "You make me want to be a better person, and I am when I'm around you. It sounds pathetic, I know, but you smile at me and I go all warm and gooey inside. I don't know what to do with that, Landon. I'm not a nice person. You said that yourself. I am *not* the warm and gooey type, for fuck's sake. That's why I can't... I just can't, okay. I'm not good boyfriend material."

Landon sighed softly, gripping his glass tightly in both hands as he stared at the fizzing brown liquid intently. "I lied before. I wouldn't be embarrassed if people thought you were my boyfriend."

"Well, obviously..." I choked a laugh out through my tears, making Landon smile too. "I mean, look at me."

"I do look at you, Rufus," he said. "A lot. The truth is, I'm happier when I'm around you too. I like being your friend, because, probably for the first time in my life, someone accepts me for who I am. That's you, Rufus. Nobody else. So maybe you're not such a horrible person after all."

"And here I was thinking I was the drunk one," I snorted.

"It's true," Landon insisted. "I don't blame you for not fancying me. I know what I look like and I know I'm not your type, but – and don't hate me for saying this – sometimes I wish I was. If I'm ever going to lose my virginity, I want it to be with you."

"I... um..." I gulped down the last of my drink and gave him what I hoped was a hard stare, but was probably more a wild, blood-shot-eyed look of sheer panic. Why was I even hesitating? Someone was offering me sex on a plate – at least I thought that was what he was doing – and I was questioning whether I should or not? And, yeah, I'd turned down guys before who didn't do anything for me, but this was Landon. Maybe the attraction I had to him was more to do with his soul than his body, but I *was* attracted, however hard I tried to fight it. "I'm no good for you, Landon."

"I'm not asking you to be. I want to go to bed with you,

not marry you." Landon took a deep breath, his gaze meeting mine across the table. "So, are we going to do this?"

"Now?"

I'd never been exactly prudish, but it was the middle of the afternoon and I was drunk. There had to be a hundred and one reasons why fucking Landon was a bad idea, most, but Little Rufus had already perked up with interest and was ignoring all of them.

Landon swallowed, suddenly awkward. "Why not? Unless you don't want to, of course. I mean... I wouldn't blame you...I know I'm..."

"Shut up, Landon," I said, standing up a little too fast so that I had to lean against the table to steady myself. "Let's go, big guy."

We stumbled drunkenly from the bar. Okay. *I* stumbled drunkenly. If Landon seemed a bit shaky on his legs, then it was for a whole different reason. The entire way back to our room, he shot me sideways looks, over and over again, like he couldn't quite believe what was happening. He practically dragged me up the stairs and through the door, as though he was afraid that, given the chance, I'd change my mind. Not that I was going to. Sex was sex. And, as it turned out, gin made me horny.

"Get undressed," I said, hopping inelegantly on one foot while I tried to pull my boot off.

Suddenly, Landon baulked, a strange look coming over his face.

"I... I don't want you to see me naked."

I stopped hopping and stared at him. I mean, I could see *why* he didn't want to get naked in front of me, but he couldn't be that naïve, could he? How the Hell did he imagine this whole scenario would play out if he didn't take his clothes off?

"Well, you can keep them on if you like," I said, "but I'm way past dry humping like teenage schoolboys and - newsflash, big man – that doesn't count as losing your virginity."

Still, he hesitated, so I decided it was time to take matters into my own hands. Pushing him back onto the bed, I stripped him of his clothes, mildly pleased to discover all that pale, flabby flesh didn't put me off quite as much as I thought it would. Either that or I was too drunk to care. I left him long enough to take off the rest of my own clothes and retrieve the necessary supplies from my overnight bag. Landon's eyes widened slightly when he saw the lube and condoms in my hand. Maybe he thought I'd brought them along with this exact moment in mind. But I hadn't brought them for him. Never imagined we'd end up like this. I always carried protection. What could I say? I was a slut.

"I don't know how to do it," Landon admitted.

"You never watched porn?"

"What? No! My parents..."

"You don't tell your parents you're watching it, idiot." I climbed up onto the bed and straddled his thighs. He trembled beneath me, but his eyes raked over my body hungrily and his impressively large dick stood to attention, letting me know he was physically still on board with getting down and dirty, even if he was having some sort of psychological crisis. "Relax, Landon. Just do what comes naturally."

I prepped myself with an ease that came from a lot of practice, while Landon watched, wide-eyed and thoroughly turned on. He palmed his dick and began to stroke it slowly. So, he'd done that much before, hopefully without needing parental supervision. When I was ready, I slapped his hand away and lowered myself carefully onto his waiting dick. Landon gasped and tensed. For a worrying moment, I thought he was going to shoot his load before I was even fully seated, but somehow he managed to hold off.

"Oh, my God, you feel... so tight," he moaned breathlessly.

"Thank you." I preened, because – let's face it – after the amount of guys I'd been with, that was a pretty huge fucking compliment. Hesitantly, Landon brought his hands to my hips. "See? I knew you'd be a natural at this."

He smiled then, his confidence growing as he tightened his grip and gave an experimental little upward thrust.

"Yeah, that feels good, baby," I encouraged.

I lifted myself almost entirely off him, braced my hands on that big belly of his, and eased back down. It didn't take long to get a rhythm going, because I knew what I was doing even if Landon didn't. The way he bucked and moaned and sweated beneath me, it was going to be one short roller-coaster ride of a fuck, so I had to get off as quick as he did. My dick bounced with every rise and fall, but Landon seemed to be so lost in chasing his own pleasure that he didn't realise he should be giving me some attention too. I took my dick into my own hand, jacking myself off as I rode him, hard and fast.

"Fuck, Rufus!"

Landon arched his back and came hard. His dick pulsed hard inside me, filling the condom and pushing me over the edge, so that I painted his chest and stomach with ropes of creamy, white cum. With a grunt, I rolled off him and stretched out on the mattress at his side. He lay there, eyes closed, panting like he'd run a marathon. I hoped he wasn't about to have a fucking heart attack or something, because I was still a little bit too drunk to cope with that kind of drama.

"That was..."

"It was okay," I interrupted quickly. He was going to trot out the usual bullshit about it being amazing, but it wasn't. He hadn't done a bad job for his first time, but I'd had better. Would hopefully have better again with men to come. Landon would have better too once he had a little more practice. "I need to sleep off the booze now. You should get cleaned up."

There was a lengthy pause before he got up from the bed and went into the bathroom. No doubt I'd heard his feelings again, but it was only a fuck. That was all. If he was looking for someone to cuddle up to after he was looking at the wrong person.

CHAPTER 11

HOURS LATER, I was awoken by a loud banging on the bedroom door. I opened my eyes and looking around, disorientated until I remembered where I was. In Weymouth for Stefan's stupid wedding and... oh, yeah, I'd let Landon fuck me. Bad move, Rufus. Very bad move. I didn't remember much about the sex, but my arse felt pleasantly sore, so it couldn't have been all bad. Landon wasn't in the room with me, which was surprising, a relief and also somewhat insulting all at the same time. I thought he'd be all clingy and shit now that we'd had sex.

There was a second volley of hammering on the door and I groaned as I rolled off the bed and went to answer. I threw open the door with a snarl, and it wasn't until I saw Killigan's shocked face that I remembered I was butt naked.

"What do you want?" I turned my back on him, stooping to retrieve my clothes from the bedroom floor. Killigan stepped inside the room and closed the door. He wrinkled his nose, which amused me immensely. "What? You don't like the smell of man sex?"

"Not particularly," he replied dryly. "But, on that note, do you really think sleeping with Landon was a good idea?"

"Honestly? No, I think it was a terrible idea, but it's not like I can take it back, is it? Where is he, anyway?"

It didn't surprise me in the slightest that Landon had told Killigan what happened. Fat idiot was probably telling anyone who'd listen, like he was staking his claim to me. Thing was, anyone who knew me, probably knew better than he did that I'd never settle for someone like him.

"He's downstairs with Marcie," Killigan answered. "In case you've forgotten, we're meeting Stefan, Alex and the others for a meal tonight. I suggest you get moving unless you want us to go without you."

"No, I'm coming." I pulled my purple boots on, ran my fingers through my hair. Hopefully, my 'just-rolled-out-of-bed' look would get Stef's attention. "I just need to clean my teeth. My mouth feels like something took a shit in there."

"I'll wait downstairs," Killigan said. "You've got ten minutes."

I made it in five, dressed in a loose purple shirt, skin-tight jeans and my purple suede boots, because I did actually want to go to this meal. Not because I wanted to help celebrate Stefan's pending nuptials, but because it was my last chance to persuade him not to go through with it. To convince him that I was the one he should be with, not that thug, Alex. Just because Stefan had got the brute partially housetrained didn't mean they would be happy together in the long run. To be honest, I wasn't sure how I was going to go about it as yet. For a start, I'd have to get him away from Alex long enough to talk to him, and I had a funny feeling everyone else would be out to prevent me from getting Stefan alone. I couldn't imagine why, but nobody seemed to trust me around him.

Landon glanced up as I entered the foyer. Hope flared on his chubby face and quickly died again when I didn't smile or give any indication that I was pleased to see him. Believe it or not, I was actually being nice; not wanting to encourage him and all that. And I knew what Killigan would say. If I didn't want to encourage him, I shouldn't have slept with him. Blah blah blah. Even Marcie gave me a look like she was disappointed in me, so I guess Landon had told her we'd fucked too. Well, I wasn't going to apologise for it; to her, Landon, or anyone else. I got drunk. I had sex. It wasn't as if I killed someone.

We all got into Killigan's car and he drove us to the restaurant where we were meeting the others. The place was small; a bit like Franco's, only classier. It was one of Stefan's favourites and because he and Alex were apparently good customers, the owner had allowed them to take over the whole restaurant for the night. No doubt, if it had been down to Alex, we'd be having this meal in the chip shop down by the old harbour.

Thanks to me and my little siesta, we were the last to arrive. Neither of the grooms had any family to speak of, but Alex's boss, Tony was there and Stefan's other best friend, Amanda, and her boyfriend. Fiancé. Whatever. I thought they were engaged, but I never usually paid that much attention to anyone or anything that didn't directly benefit me in some way. I'd known Amanda for years without ever really getting to *know* her. Eric sat in a corner, talking quietly with Mason. How awkward was that? Being in the same room with the ex and his new shag? He looked happy though, which was slightly annoying. I liked to think he would have missed me just a bit. There were other people too that I didn't recognise, but Marcie had told me before we came that they'd invited work colleagues and a few people from Stefan's college course.

Unsurprisingly, Stefan was the only one who actually seemed pleased to see me. Throwing his arms around my neck, he kissed me on the lips, which got raised eyebrows from Landon. Thankfully Alex was on the other side of the room and didn't notice. He was possessive over Stefan at the best of times, but especially when it came to me. Maybe, despite that thick brain of his, he saw me for the threat I really was. That was a good thing though. If Alex saw me as a threat, then it had to mean I had a chance with Stefan.

"Who's your friend?" Stefan asked, eyeing Landon curiously.

"Nobody," I said, dismissing Landon with a flick of my hand. "Listen, Stefan, are you–?"

"Please don't ask me if I'm sure." Stefan's smile slipped. "I'm marrying Alex. Tomorrow. And we are *not* having this conversation again."

"Fine."

There was still time to work on changing his mind. Not much, admittedly, but all I had to do was get him on his own. The restaurant was probably a bit public anyway. Too many disapproving faces staring at us.

"Come and say hello to Alex," Stefan said brightly, grabbing hold of my hand.

I rolled my eyes. "Do I have to?"

"Yes, you do." He scowled at me, but there was a sparkle in his eye that told me he wasn't really angry. "Bring your boyfriend."

"He's not my boyfriend, Stefan," I reminded him as he dragged me across the restaurant, Landon trailing miserably behind us.

"Alex, baby, look who's here."

Even before Alex had fully turned to face us, Stefan spotted someone he just *had* to say hello to and he was gone. Alex and I stared at each other awkwardly. On the surface, we tolerated each other these days for Stefan's sake, but he didn't like me anymore than I liked him and that was probably never going to change. In fact, if I ever succeeded in getting Stefan away from him, I had no doubt Alex would quite happily kill me with his bare hands and not even feel guilty about it.

"Rufus," he said stiffly. At least he called me by my actual name now. That was progress, I supposed. "Who's your friend?" His eyes narrowed as he looked at Landon. "Wait, don't I know you from some place? You look familiar."

"Yes, I think we met a few months ago at that pub on the seafront," Landon said shyly. "I'm Landon."

"Landon. That's it." Alex reached out and shook Landon's hand, smiling at him warmly. I frowned. Alex had never reacted to me in that way, so I was like *'what the fuck?'* Landon and Alex had met before? And Alex liked him?

"What? So, you two know each other?" I asked, glaring from one to the other suspiciously. "How? Since when?"

"It was when Stef was in London," Alex explained.

"And I told you my family came here for my sister's birthday," Landon added.

"Right, but how did you meet Alex?" I demanded, unreasonably angry.

"We both happened to be at the pub," Alex answered. "We got talking, that's all."

"Talking?" I arched an eyebrow. "A few months ago? You mean when Stefan left you?" I folded my arms and glowered at Alex. "And does Stefan know that while he was going through hell, you were out on the pull?"

"It wasn't like that," Landon protested.

"And you... giving me all that bullshit about being a virgin. Oh, poor me," I mimicked. "I'm so fat and ugly no one will fuck me. Did he use that line on you too, Alex?"

"Shut your damn mouth," Alex hissed furiously, glancing around to see if anyone was standing close enough to have overheard. "Don't go stirring shit up, Rufus. Not the night before my fucking wedding."

"So, Stefan doesn't know," I said, feeling absolutely triumphant. I had the bastard. After all this time, I actually had him.

"There's nothing *to* know. I'm warning you, Rufus, don't even think about saying anything to Stef."

"Hey, what are you guys talking about?" Stefan bounced back over to where we were standing and linked his arm through Alex's. He didn't seem to pick up on the tension between me and his soon-to-be husband. Or, more likely, he was ignoring, not wanting the aggravation right before his wedding. He was used to me and Alex being at each other's throats. "I think everyone is here now, so we should take our seats."

We joined the others at the tables and I was annoyed to find I was sat about as far away from Stefan as I could get while still being in the same room. Maybe we didn't see each other every day like we used to, but I was still supposed to be his best friend. Yet my place at his side seemed to have been taken by casual acquaintances and work colleagues who couldn't begin to know him even half as well as I did. It wasn't fair. I was being pushed out, and now I knew Alex's dirty little secret it was obvious why. Alex knew if

Stefan found out he'd cheated, he'd lose him and I'd win.

Killigan was right next to Alex, like he was the father of the bride or something. Eric and Mason – who, for the record, hadn't bothered to come and say hello – were there too. If it wasn't for me, neither of them would know Stefan and Alex in the first place, so how come they were sat closer to Stefan than I was?

The food wasn't bad, but I'd let my bad mood affect my appetite and I really wasn't hungry. Landon made more than one attempt to initiate conversation, all of which I resolutely ignored.

At the end of the meal, Killigan insisted on making a speech, something I thought was ridiculously unnecessary given that he'd probably say the exact same words at the wedding the next day. The whole evening was a complete waste of time in my opinion.

"I've got something to say." I stopped Killigan mid-flow and took a big swallow of the sweet, sickly wine they'd served with the meal before I got to my feet.

"Rufus, what are you doing?" Killigan asked, not best pleased by my interruption. Whatever. My speech was going to be way more interesting than his anyway.

"Sweetheart, are you sure this is a good idea?"

That was Marcie for you; forever playing the role of peacekeeper. In the end though, she'd side with her precious bloody Alex, just like she always did.

"Better now than after he marries him," I said loudly, ensuring I had the attention of everyone sat around the table. Stefan was staring at me, eyes wide with confusion, while Alex looked about ready to commit murder. Not that I was going to let that stop me. "Alex cheated on you," I blurted out. "When you were in London a few months ago, all that shit you were going through with your dad, Alex didn't care. He slept with Landon."

"Rufus, stop it." Eric barely raised his voice, but he didn't have to. His outrage was right there in his tone. "Just shut up and sit down."

"You don't get to tell me what to do anymore," I snapped at him. "Not since you left me for your meathead boyfriend. Remind me, Eric, what is it you see in the rich and famous Mace White?"

"For fuck's sake, Rufus." Alex leapt to his feet, his expression thunderous. "I swear to God, one more word and I'll–"

"Alex." Stefan reached up and put his hand on Alex's arm. One softly spoken word, one gentle touch, and the mighty beast was instantly tamed. I smirked, delighted that Stefan was so quick to defend me. "I'm sorry I can't do this anymore. I think you should leave."

"Yeah, off you go," I sneered, hardly able to believe my luck. This was really happening. Alex was out of the picture and it was only a matter of time until Stefan was finally mine. "Wedding's off, bozo."

"Not him." Stefan switched his gaze from Alex to me, and I saw the tears brimming in his eyes. "You, Rufus. You're the one who needs to leave. And don't bother coming to the wedding tomorrow. You're uninvited."

"You're not serious? I just told you he cheated on you, Stefan." I looked around the table, expecting to find a modicum of support from at least a couple of the other guests. Most of them wouldn't even look at me though, and those that met my gaze did so with shock, anger and disgust on their faces. Obviously, there would be no back up coming from any of that bunch of losers. "You know what?" I spat. "If you're stupid enough to stay with him, then you deserve everything you get. Don't come crying to me when he screws you over yet again. Come on, Landon. We're leaving."

Landon gawped at me, open mouthed, and made no move to get up out of his seat.

"Landon is staying with us," Killigan said firmly.

I didn't bother arguing. It wasn't like I wanted him to go with me anyway. I turned on my heel and flounced out of the restaurant. Outside, two things suddenly occurred to me. The first was that I had no idea where I was or how I was going to get back to the hotel.

The second was that I might just have made a terrible mistake.

CHAPTER 12

I DID MAKE it back to the hotel, of course, although it took a while. During the long chilly walk, I realised the one person I had hurt most of all was myself. The sick feeling in the pit of my stomach had nothing to do with Stefan throwing me out and everything to do with Landon's refusal to come with me. I wasn't sure what that meant? Why would I be more upset about losing Landon than I was Stefan?

And that was when it hit me. I needed Landon in my life more than I needed Stefan. Yes, I loved Stefan, but it was as a brother rather than a potential lover. He'd moved on with Alex years ago and, much as I hated to admit it, they were happy together. Maybe it *was* time to let him go and end my stupid vendetta against Alex once and for all.

Even if I did though, it wouldn't resolve the problem I'd caused with Landon. I liked Landon. Life was better with him in it. *I* was better when he was around. I was happier. I'd fallen for the big man without even realising it. At least, the new and improved Rufus had. Pity then, that I'd relapsed into the old and emotionally lacking Rufus in such dramatic fashion and blown our friendship straight to Hell.

Sitting on the side of the bed in the hotel, I waited for Landon to come back to our room, hoping he'd give me the chance to make things right. In the early hours of the morning I realised that he wasn't going to show at all. Not that I blamed him, I supposed. By claiming Alex had slept with Landon, I'd dragged Landon into the whole messy situation and embarrassed him greatly. He was bound to be hurt and angry and I understood why he would be, but surely he'd see that everything I'd done was to stop my best friend from marrying the wrong man? Thing was, I didn't even believe that myself anymore. I knew Alex and Landon hadn't slept together, but I'd seen my chance and run with it, without stopping to consider the consequences. I hadn't cared what it would do to Landon and – when I really thought about it – I hadn't cared how much it would hurt Stefan either. Fuck, I'd been so stupid. I didn't know if there was any way of coming back from this with any of them.

Eventually, I slept, fully clothed, without bothering to crawl beneath the bedcovers, only to be woken what felt like mere minutes, but was actually four or five hours later, by a loud and repeated banging on the bedroom door. I sat bolt upright, my heart pounding almost as much as whoever was hammering on the door. I tried to convince myself it would be Landon, but he'd never make that much noise and draw attention to himself, besides which he had a key. Killigan then, come to tell me to make my own way back to London, pack up my stuff and get the hell out of his house before he got home. But no, there was only one person who knocked on a door like he was trying to break it down and that was Alex Gill.

Still, I'd known for a long time that this moment was

coming. Finally, he was going to do what I'd accused him of doing from the beginning and beat the shit out of me. Thing was, I felt unbelievably calm and accepting of my fate, because this time I deserved it. This time it wasn't about being gay. It was about being a complete bastard. I threw back my shoulders and took several deep breaths, before crossing the room and throwing open the door. Alex stood head and shoulders above me and was probably twice as wide. I had to tilt my head back to look him in the eye.

"Shouldn't you be at a wedding?"

"That's later, dickhead," Alex snapped, pushing past me and into the bedroom. "Why doesn't it surprise me you don't even know what time the ceremony takes place?"

"So, are you here to beat me up?" I asked, my bravado slipping slightly, because I really didn't cope well with pain. I didn't even like rough sex. "I know I deserve it after what I did last night."

"Damn fucking right you deserve it." Alex sat on the edge of the bed and glared at me. "But, even though Stef's angry with you, he'd never forgive me if I did anything to you."

"Why are you here then?"

"I don't know. To talk?"

"Talk?" I echoed like I'd never heard the word before. Jesus, a conversation with Alex was potentially more painful than him bashing me.

"Yeah, you know... like with words and stuff."

"Right... um..." I wrung my hands together in front of my chest and looked at him helplessly. "So... who goes first?"

"Well, you, obviously, seeing as you're the one who doesn't give a fuck who you hurt so long as you split up me and Stef."

"I... I..." Suddenly I found it hard to speak around the lump in my throat. I blinked rapidly, but the blur in my wet eyes refused to clear.

"Don't bother," Alex said from the bed. "If it doesn't work on me when Stef cries, it sure as shit won't when you do it."

I dashed my hands to my eyes in an attempt to stem the flow of tears, but it was too late. The well of emotion in my chest overflowed and poured from my open mouth in a long, wail of absolute anguish.

"Everyone hates me!" I howled dramatically. "I'm a horrible person. You... you should punch me. Right now. In the face... I... I..."

"Oh, for fuck's sake." Alex got to his feet, sounding more exasperated than sympathetic. "Get your shoes on."

"Wh... why?" I snivelled, rubbing my eyes. "Where are... are we going?"

"I'm taking you out for breakfast. So, hurry up. I haven't got all day."

I wasn't in the least bit hungry, but I pulled on my boots and ran my fingers through my messy hair before following Alex from the room and down the hallway, still blubbing and wiping my nose on the sleeve of my shirt. The drive was a silent one and thankfully short. Alex drove us down to Bowleaze Cove and the café there that looked out over the serene waters of the bay.

It was still early so the café was fairly quiet there were only two or three older couples, dog walkers or ramblers I supposed, and a family with two small kids, all of whom seemed to be currently enjoying their breakfasts. I didn't look at any of them too closely and hoped they didn't look at me either. I'm sure they did though. We must have made a sight, Alex and me. The musclebound man-mountain and the skinny short-arse with purple hair.

"Get a table," Alex said pointing through an open archway to a light, airy conservatory seating area. "I'll order."

The conservatory was empty, so I chose a table at the back, forsaking the breath-taking sea view for a secluded spot out of view of the curious gazes of the other diners. And still I couldn't stop fucking crying. Not the heartfelt sobs of before maybe, but my damn eyes refused to stop leaking and every minute or so I hiccupped a deep, shuddery breath.

Alex joined me a few minutes later and placed a gently steaming mug of hot chocolate in front of me, whipped cream and chocolate sprinkles and all. Marcie had taught him well. I wrapped my hands around the mug and sniffed. He dropped into a chair on the opposite side of the table and scowled.

"Will you please stop crying? Everybody out there already thinks I'm abusing you."

"Sorry," I muttered, lowering my head so he wouldn't see the fresh swell of tears. "It's just... I messed everything up. He's never going to forgive me. Not this time."

Alex sighed. "He's angry, right now, yeah, but Stef loves you. As a brother," he added quickly. "He'll forgive you eventually.

"Not Stefan," I said tearfully. "Landon."

"Landon?"

Alex couldn't hide his surprise, but before he could say anything though, our breakfast arrived, a large full English for Alex and a smaller serving for me. It was my turn to raise my eyebrows, because who knew Alex Gill had it in him to be so considerate? The café owner glanced from my blotchy face to Alex suspiciously, but any notion he had to interfere disintegrated rapidly beneath the intensity of Alex's challenging glare.

As soon as the guy left us alone again, Alex tucked into his breakfast enthusiastically. Realising I was hungrier than I first thought, I picked up my cutlery and started on my own plate of food. The bacon was nice and crispy, exactly the way I liked it.

"So... talk," Alex said around a mouthful of baked beans and fried bread. "Make me understand."

I glanced at him across the table. "Understand what?"

"Start with why you tried to split me and Stef up. *Again.*"

"I don't know. Habit, I guess. I spent so long convincing myself that Stefan would be better off with me than with you, that I didn't know how to stop."

"Because you want Stef for yourself," Alex stated.

I glanced at him again, but nothing about him seemed immediately threatening. He didn't even seem angry.

"I thought I did," I admitted. "I mean, I do love him, but not the way you do. I can see that now."

"Okay, so what changed since yesterday?"

I shrugged. "I don't know."

You do know, a little voice nagged at the back of my head. And it was right, I did know. Landon was what happened. Losing him hurt far more than the prospect of losing Stefan. I still wasn't ready though, to admit it to myself, let alone Alex Gill.

"Try this then. What do you want out of life, Rufus?"

"Same as everybody else," I answered. "I want to be happy."

"Okay. What else?"

"I want Killigan to like me. For him to look at me like he doesn't have a bad smell under his nose for once."

Alex laughed. "Yeah, I can agree with you on that one. In case you hadn't noticed, he's not exactly my biggest fan either. What else?"

"I want Marcie to love me and call me one of her boys like she does with you and Stefan."

"She already does. You're a fucking idiot if you don't see it. What else?"

I knew what he was trying to get me to tell him, but still I resisted.

"Um... well, I want to be a chef. Turns out I'm quite a good cook, so..."

"You're really going to make me drag it out of you, aren't you?"

"I... I don't know what you mean."

Alex grinned at me. "You like Landon."

"I... I can't... it's just..." Suddenly I was no longer hungry. I pushed away the remains of my breakfast in frustration. "I can't believe I'm having this conversation, with you of all people. I'm different when I'm around Landon. I'm a better person because being with him makes me want to *be* better. I don't expect you to believe me, especially after last night, but I'm nicer when I'm with Landon. Being with him makes me the happiest I've probably ever been in my whole life."

Alex leaned back in his chair and stared at me, his expression serious. Whether he actually believed me or not I didn't know, but he was listening at least.

"Then what's the problem?" he asked. "Why ruin what you have with Landon with what you did yesterday?"

"Because I always ruin everything," I said, feeling the tears prick my eyes again. I rubbed them away furiously, determined not to resume my earlier sob-fest. "I try, I really do. But every time it feels like we're getting closer, I panic. I start thinking what people will say about me and him. That they'll look at us and laugh at us because he's so fat. And do you know what? His size doesn't even bother me, it really doesn't. It's just part of who he is. But you know me, I'm all about the public image and I can't stand to think people are laughing at me because of Landon. So, I push him away and then I miss him and pull him back in again. It's such a fucking mess."

"And then some," Alex agreed.

"Shit." I flopped forward to rest my forehead against the cool surface of the table with a long groan. "What am I going to do?"

"Well, first of all, you should probably get your hair out of the bean juice," Alex said, sounding highly amused. I sat up abruptly, scowling when the thick orange liquid dripped from my fringe and rolled down my nose. Alex grinned at me again. "Good look. It suits you. Okay, after I drop you back at the hotel, you're going to shower, get yourself all dollied up – head to toe in fucking purple, no doubt – and then you're going to get yourself to the wedding for three o'clock. I take it you know where?"

"Yeah, that big hotel overlooking the bay." I rolled my eyes at him. "But you're forgetting something. Stefan uninvited me."

"Then I'm un-uninviting you. Trust me, Stef will be fine with it."

"Stefan maybe," I said grudgingly. "I'm not so sure about Landon."

"You need to prove to him that you're serious about him. You're going to have to grovel big time." Alex smirked at me. "I can't wait to see it."

CHAPTER 13

NAKED AND IN the shower while thinking about Alex Gill was a new and rather disconcerting experience. Trouble was, I couldn't get him off my mind. Not to say that I suddenly fancied him or anything, because *that* was most definitely never going to happen. It was that I'd never really known he was... well... kind of *nice*. He'd shown sympathy, understanding and a level of concern that I would never have thought him capable of. As well as that, he seemed quietly intelligent. Not in a rocket scientist way or anything, but there was more going on behind those big brown eyes than most people, including me, ever gave him credit for. If I pulled this off, got everyone to forgive me and convinced Landon that I wanted us to be proper boyfriends – then I might actually end up liking the big goon.

The one thing that worried me slightly, was that while I had been out with Alex, it looked as though Landon had been back to the room and taken his overnight bag. I wondered if Alex had been a decoy, sent to get me out of the way so that Landon could get his stuff without having to see me, but then Alex had seemed so genuine. If it was all some clever ruse, he wouldn't have invited me to the wedding, would he?

Once I'd showered and washed the sticky bean juice from my hair, I dressed in my new outfit, white drainpipe jeans and a deep purple button-down shirt matched with my purple suede ankle-boots. I gelled my hair into soft purple spikes and applied glittery purple eyeshadow, eyeliner and mascara. I wasn't trying to outshine the bride – or groom, whatever Stefan was calling himself – because even at my best I could never compete with Stefan's much more natural beauty. I had to make the effort though. I had my own man to snare and I had to look good enough to get his attention from the moment I walked in.

I took a taxi to the hotel, which turned out to be a little further up the road from where Alex and I had had breakfast that morning. There were more people milling around waiting for the ceremony to start than I expected. It made me wonder who they all were, because Alex and Stefan didn't really do the friend thing. They always seemed happy in their own little world, and it was like they didn't need anyone else in their lives. I'd thought, at first, booking the hotel was overkill and that it would only be the usual gang, me, Killigan, Marcie, Amanda and her fiancé, and then Eric and Mason since they'd all become best buddies after Eric and I split up. Then there was their old landlord, Tony, but that was still only eight people. There had to be fifty or more people in this one room, although there was no sign of Alex, Stefan, Killigan or Tony.

"Rufus!"

I turned with a nervous smile as Marcie swept across the floor towards me, looking stunning in a summery floral dress and smelling of light, sweet perfume. I always joked that if I was straight and twenty years older, I would have made a play for her myself. She gathered me up in her arms and kissed my cheek.

"I'm so happy you decided to come, sweetheart."

"Alex said it would be okay," I said quickly, suddenly anxious she would think I'd turned up uninvited to cause more trouble. "Are you... are you angry with me? For last night?"

"I'm absolutely furious," she told me, cupping my face in her hands. "And, let me assure you, Rufus, we *will* be discussing your behaviour when we get home, but for now... let's just enjoy the wedding, eh?"

I nodded, pathetically grateful that she was prepared to be so understanding. Somehow, I doubted Killigan would wait until we got home before he started in on me. If he didn't tear me a new one at the reception, he was bound to start as soon as we got in the car to go home.

"Have you... I mean... is Landon here?"

"Oh, sweetie, you really like him, don't you?" Marcie smiled sympathetically. "He's out on the terrace. Go on, hurry up and tell him how sorry you are. I know he'll be pleased to see you."

She hugged me again, before pushing me in the direction of a set of open French doors that I assumed led out onto the terrace.

There were a few more people out there, enjoying the late afternoon sun as they chatted. Landon was on the far side of the terrace, looking out towards the sea. I assumed he was alone because... well, he was Landon and I was pretty much the only friend he had. But then he moved and I saw there was someone with him. Someone small and slim with messy ink-black hair and intense, bright blue eyes. I thought Stefan was beautiful, but this kid put even him to shame. In truth, he was stunning. Stunning and smiling up at my would-be boyfriend with his stupid perfect lips and stupid perfect straight, white teeth.

He looked like a tramp though, like he was some home-less person who'd just wandered in off the street. Honestly, it was a wonder the hotel hadn't thrown him out. He couldn't be a guest, because nobody went to a wedding dressed in a t-shirt three sizes too big for them, faded leggings with holes in the knees and... bare feet. He had bare feet! Trust Landon and his big heart to take pity on a passing stray, although bringing him to the wedding seemed a bit inappropriate. I would have thought Landon had the intelligence to realise that it was a bad idea.

I stalked over to them and put a possessive hand on Landon's arm at the same time as glaring at the drop-dead-gorgeous young man. Landon looked at me in surprise, but he didn't pull away which had to be a good sign that I was forgiven.

"Rufus! I wasn't sure if you'd come."

"Well, I did," I said, looking the black-haired kid up and down and making it clear I found him wanting. "Who's your friend?"

"This is Sunny," he said. "He's at college with your friend Stefan."

"N-nice to m-meet you," Sunny said, sounding friendly enough even though he eyed me warily.

"N-nice to m-meet you too," I mimicked. "Now f-fuck off."

He looked at me like he was about to burst into tears or something, then he turned tail and ran. I watched him go with a smirk and then realised Landon was staring at me with such a furious expression that I took an involuntary step backwards.

"That was cruel and unnecessary," he snapped, his tone

angrier than I'd ever heard him use on me or anyone else in the entire time I'd known him. "What did you have to do that for? He didn't do anything to you."

"Oh, come on," I said with an impatient roll of my eyes. "Don't tell me you didn't notice he was hot as fuck. He can easily go get his own boyfriend, looking like that. He doesn't have to go chasing after mine."

Landon's jaw literally dropped and he looked at me in disbelief.

"There is so much wrong with what you just said that I don't even know where to start."

I shrugged. "Just telling it as it is."

"Rufus, I..." Landon threw his hands in the air in exasperation. "Okay, first of all, yes, of course I noticed he's hot. I'd have to be blind not to. But you know what else I saw? Behind those flawless features, I saw a damaged soul. Someone who's broken and hurting."

"Right," I said scornfully. "Did he tell you that himself?"

"No, Rufus, I saw the scars on his arms, some of them fresh. They're the kind of scars that only come from self-harm."

"I never saw anything," I muttered defensively, because if I was honest, I hadn't looked at him beyond his perfect face and the rags that he wore. But self-harm? That was some serious shit and I did feel a little bit guilty. Nobody would believe me even if I said it, but I hoped my snarky little comment to him hadn't driven him to do anything stupid. "Landon, I know I–"

"Secondly," Landon cut in hotly, "he has a boyfriend. Sunny didn't say as much, but I get the impression the boyfriend's married and that's why he's not here."

"Okay, I'm sorry, I just–"

"And thirdly," Landon interrupted again. "I'm not your boyfriend, Rufus. After the way you've behaved so far this weekend, I wouldn't even want to be. You made it quite clear last night that it's Stefan you want to be with. Not me."

"I know, but I was wrong," I said desperately, because without even meaning to, I'd slipped back into the old Rufus and completely blown what was meant to be my heartfelt apology and a declaration of romantic interest; and all because I'd let my jealousy get the better of me. "You're the one I like. I want to give it a go between us. See what happens."

"You're only saying that because Stefan chose Alex and not you. I'm not some sort of consolation prize, Rufus."

"No, I know. I'm not saying that. Give me one more chance. Let me prove to you that I mean it this time."

"How many last chances am I supposed to give you?" Landon asked with a little shake of his head. "Every time I let you in, start to trust you, you hurt me all over again. I'm not doing it anymore. I think it would be best if you left me alone for a bit. I have some thinking to do."

He turned away and began to walk away, his head hanging low.

"Landon."

He looked back over his shoulder with troubled brown eyes.

"We're still friends though, right?"

"You want the truth, Rufus?" Landon said sadly. "I really don't know anymore."

I watched him go, telling myself that he didn't mean it. Because he didn't, did he? He couldn't. He liked me too much to walk away from whatever this was between us without a backward glance. We worked together too, so what did he think was going to happen there? If he decided he didn't want to see me at all anymore, would he quit his job to avoid me? That was the last thing I wanted to happen, because if he left the restaurant, I'd never have the chance to atone for the numerous mistakes I'd made with him.

I found myself facing quite the dilemma. On the one hand, I wanted the old Landon back. The original painfully shy, quietly spoken, massively overweight man who I could wrap around my little finger. On the other hand, I was proud of the man he'd become. He was stronger, more confident in himself. And, although he would probably still be classed by the medical profession as morbidly obese, he *had* lost weight. I didn't even know if I'd like him as much if he ended up as slim as me and Stefan. Obviously, he needed to be a healthier weight than he was currently, but his size was a part of him. It worried me that he wouldn't be the same Landon and if he changed too much, he wouldn't like me anymore.

Okay, okay. So, technically he didn't like me that much at the moment as it was, but I still held out hope that he wouldn't be angry with me forever.

"Rufus, sweetheart." Marcie appeared in front of me, her face sympathetic. I guess she'd figured out by the fact I was stood on the terrace alone that my attempt to win Landon back hadn't gone too well. "The ceremony's starting soon. Are you coming in?"

"Of course." I plastered a fake smile on my face. "Let's go and get my best friend married."

CHAPTER 14

INSIDE, most of the seats were already full. Given a choice, I would have hidden away at the back in case Stefan was annoyed that I'd shown up to the ceremony despite him banning me. Marcie wouldn't stand for it though and dragged me up to the front row next to her and Amanda and her boyfriend. Amanda glared at me, leaving me in no doubt as to her feelings about me. I felt a hand slip into mine and give an encouraging squeeze. Turning away from Amanda's silent disapproval, I was met with Marcie's warm smile and I relaxed a little.

The rows of chairs on either side of the room formed a narrow aisle, of which Alex stood at the head, his boss, Tony, at his side acting as best man. It had to be said, Alex looked incredibly handsome in a charcoal grey suit over an open-neck black shirt. He also looked uncharacteristically nervous, glancing repeatedly over his shoulder toward the door through which Stefan would come. During one of those backward glances his gaze met mine. He didn't smile, but he nodded and then mouthed *thank you*, before his eyes flicked back to the door.

Stefan, I had to admit, looked pretty fucking amazing. I should have known he'd go down the blushing bride route, although he had stopped short of wearing a dress. His suit was white though, complimenting his blond hair perfectly. He beamed proudly, his eyes bright and full of love as he walked up the aisle on Killigan's arm. I tensed as they got nearer, afraid Stefan might object to my being there, but the fact of the matter was he didn't even notice me. He didn't have eyes for anybody but the man waiting for him in front of the altar.

The celebrant was a trendy looking woman in her early fifties, short and plump, and with an infectious smile that relaxed everyone almost instantly, and the service was short but nice. Kind of sweet actually. They'd written their own vows. Stefan's brought a tear to more than one eye in the room, while Alex's made everyone laugh. Even me, although I had a suspicion that he hadn't set out to be intentionally funny.

At the end, when Stefan and Alex were pronounced husband and husband, I found myself clapping and cheering along with everyone else. Funny thing was I wasn't even a little bit jealous. Well... maybe a little bit, not because Alex had Stefan, but because they had each other. I wanted that kind of relationship for myself. Stefan caught my eye and smiled, letting me know I was forgiven.

While Alex and Stefan were busy doing the official signing of paperwork bit of the proceedings, I twisted around to see where Landon had got to. He was a few rows back, sat on the other side of the aisle from me with that damn weird kid at his side. They were talking, about something serious too if the matching expressions on their faces were anything to go by. Landon glanced up, frowning when he caught me watching him. He looked away again. No smile. No nod. No nothing.

Marcie laid her hand on my arm and I turned back to look at her.

"Sweetheart, you need to put things right there, before you lose him for good."

"I tried," I said miserably. "And I just made things worse. He said he doesn't even want to be my friend."

"Give him some time and space," Marcie encouraged, giving my arm a little squeeze. "But not too much of either or someone else will snap him up."

I swivelled round again to look at Landon, Marcie's words making me see him in a new light. He had changed in the time I'd known him, and despite being the new and improved me, I'd still been too selfish to notice. He was still a pretty big guy, but he had lost more weight than I gave him credit for. He'd cut his hair too and now sported a shorter style that was much better suited to his heavy features. He looked healthier. More confident. And maybe it was down to his friendship with me or maybe he'd have done it anyway, but he seemed to have come out of his shell a lot more. People liked him. Far more than they ever liked me. In a way I was pleased for him, but Marcie was right. I wasn't the only one who was new and improved around here. Landon was too and people had started to notice. It was only a matter of time before some creep took a romantic interest in him.

Shit. That was something else Marcie was right about. I had to put things right before I lost him to somebody who was nicer to him, respected him more, and treated him better than I ever could.

I tried getting closer to him at the reception, but Landon was having none of it. Anytime I got anywhere near, he'd find some feeble excuse to move away or go and talk to a complete stranger or get another drink from the bar, even if he had a full glass in hand. And everywhere he went that stupidly gorgeous kid with the black hair and bright sapphire eyes followed close behind. It wasn't like he was hitting on Landon or anything, but I still wished he'd do me a favour and fuck off for five minutes.

At least Alex was enjoying my humiliation. They all were. All of them watching me and – aside from Marcie who looked concerned – unable to hide their smirks every time I got knocked back. Eventually, I ended up standing at the bar next to Alex, my old arch nemesis and – for some strange reason – apparently also my new best friend.

"Wow, all this time I thought you were a player," he said, "but you really suck at this romance shit, don't you? He'd rather be with that little freak, Sunny, than with you."

"I'm trying," I grumbled, scanning the room for Landon for about the billionth time.

"Try harder." Alex took a mouthful of beer, staring at me over the rim of the glass as he did. "Seriously, Doofus, you're blowing this big time. I don't know what's happened to the pushy, self-centred dick you've always been, but you might want to bring him back just long enough to grow a fucking pair and go and tell Landon you love him."

"I never said anything about love," I said, feeling suddenly flustered.

"Yeah, but you do, so go and sort it out, moron, before he elopes with bloody Sunny."

I left Alex smirking into his beer and hurried outside, because if Landon and Sunny were not inside then they had to be out on the terrace doing God knows what. If they were getting down and dirty when I found them, I wasn't sure what I'd do. Probably throw a massive hissy fit, cry for a bit, and then go back to being the complete arsehole I'd always been before I met Landon. What was the point in trying to act like a decent human being if the one person you were doing it for went off with someone else?

Fortunately for me, and I guess for everyone who had to live with me, I didn't find them canoodling in a corner. They weren't even together. Of Landon, there was no sign. Sunny stood on his own at the very edge of the terrace, watching in apparent fascination as he wiggled his own toes in the grass. He looked up when he heard someone approaching, letting out a small squeak of fright when he saw it was me. I raised my hands, palms outward in surrender before he could run away. I could see in his eyes that was what he wanted to do.

"Wait, please. Don't go." He stilled, ice-blue eyes watching me warily. "I'm sorry about before, okay? I shouldn't have taken the piss," I continued. "I was acting like a jealous idiot."

His eyes widened slightly in realisation. "L-l-landon?" he asked stiffly. "Y-you like him?"

"Yeah, I do. And I've been too fucking blind to see it. I don't suppose you know where he is?"

Sunny's bright-eyed gaze studied me intently for a moment and then he pointed. I noticed the myriad of scars on his arms that Landon had mentioned; some of them faded and silver, others raised and pink. He caught me looking and dropped his arm to his side so that scars were hidden from view.

"B-b-beach," he ground out awkwardly.

"Thank you. And... sorry again. I didn't mean to be a dick to you. Well... I did mean it, but I still shouldn't have done it. So, yeah... sorry."

He nodded stiffly and then scurried away, making sure

to give the other guests on the terrace a wide berth. And people thought *I* was strange.

Now to find Landon and put things right with him. God, all this apologising was exhausting.

"Rufus, sweetie." Marcie appeared at my side, smiling as always. "Eric and Mason are leaving. They have to get back to Pittsburgh for the next leg of Mason's tour. Don't you want to come and say goodbye?"

Quite frankly, I didn't. I'd much rather go and find Landon than face my ex and his musclebound boyfriend. But Marcie was looking at me expectantly and I just couldn't say no to the woman after everything she'd done for me.

Inside, Eric and Mason were stood in a group consisting of Stefan and Alex, Killigan, Tony, Amanda and Dan. It was like a meeting of the official people-who-hate-Rufus club. A couple of them glared in my direction as Marcie joined them. Eric shot Mason a resigned look and then split away from the group, walking across the room to meet me halfway.

"Are you okay?" he asked gruffly. He was a decent enough guy that – even though he was angry with me and probably hated that he cared – the fact was he *did* still care what happened to me.

"I will be. I know I messed up big time, Eric, but I'm trying to make things right."

"Yeah, well... if Alex and Stefan can forgive you for that dick move that you made last night, then I suppose I can." He sighed heavily. "You know, I always knew you loved Stefan more than you loved me, but I never imagined you'd go as far as you did..."

"I didn't!" I said quickly. "Love him more than you, I mean. I loved you both in my own way. Trouble is, I totally suck at it and my way turns out to be the shittiest way ever."

Eric shook his head and chuckled. "You might be right about that. This Landon guy, though... you like him, right?"

I shrugged, trying to portray an air of indifference and failing miserably. Eric could see straight through me.

"I already fucked up too badly. I don't think he'll forgive me for last night, even if everyone else does."

"Well, then you have to try harder to make it up to him. That's if you really like him and want to be with him."

"I do," I said honestly, not surprised by the doubt that flashed across Eric's face. He'd seen Landon and he knew me well enough to know it went against my nature to even be friends with someone like that. "I'm different when I'm with him, Eric. He makes me a better person. Then I have to go and do something stupid like relapsing into the old me and driving him away when I need him."

I needed him? I didn't think I'd ever said that about anybody in my life before. Not even Stefan. And what did it even mean? What did I need him for exactly? To be happier? To be a nicer person? To balance me out? All of the above?

"Tell you what," Eric said, "Mason's band are doing a show over here next month. Why don't you bring Landon? I'll have to talk to Mason, but I'm sure I can get you tickets."

"Really? That would be amazing." I didn't know why he would do something like that for me. Not only was he my ex, but after I threw him out of our apartment, he'd learned exactly how many times I'd cheated him while we were together. Well, I say *exactly*. It was more like roughly. Suffice to say it was more than the two occasions I'd told him about. Eric really was the most decent guy I'd ever met. "Oh, my God. Thank you. I can't wait to tell Landon."

"Hold on." Eric laughed at my enthusiasm. "I have to talk to Mason first. I'll call you, okay?"

"Yeah, okay," I grumbled, because patience was hardly one of my biggest virtues at the best of times. "Can I go now?"

"You don't have to ask my permission, Rufus." Eric laughed again. "Christ, you never did it the whole time we were together, so you don't need to start now. Maybe Landon really is a good influence on you."

I hurried away, not bothering to say goodbye to Mason. It wasn't like I'd ever really spoken to him anyway and I was well aware of the fact he didn't entirely approve of the fact Eric and I had stayed in touch. Outside again, I made my way across the terrace and the lawns, looking for a path that led down to the beach.

My only hope was that Landon would be there and that he'd listen to me. That he'd give me one more last chance to show him I could be the boyfriend he deserved.

CHAPTER 15

LANDON STOOD ALONE at the water's edge. He'd taken his socks and shoes off and held the hems of his trouser-legs up above the breakers that rolled over his feet. I kept my distance, not wanting to risk getting wet. Suede boots and sea water were *not* a good combination. I could take them off, I supposed, but my jeans were too tight to roll up and I really didn't want them to be ruined either. So, I stayed where I was, quietly thankful that the beach on this side of the bay was shingle rather than sand, because that would play havoc with my beautiful boots as well. And, yes, I knew I should be worrying more about Landon than my outfit, but my clothes were important to me too.

At the same time as fretting over the welfare of my outfit, I watched Landon enjoying his paddling session. He was lost in his own thoughts and totally oblivious to the fact I was behind him. It was nice – quiet and peaceful – just the two of us on that little section of the beach. Together but not together. I felt more relaxed than I had done for a long time. I could have called out to him and let him know I was there, but there was a part of me that didn't want to spoil the moment. I still couldn't be sure how he was going to react to me.

Finally, after ten minutes or so, Landon turned away from the water. His eyes widened slightly when he saw me standing there, but he didn't smile. He walked a short way up the beach and lowered his bulk onto the shingle so that he could put his socks and shoes back on. I waited for him to say something, suddenly nervous. What if he decided not to forgive me as willingly as everyone else had? What did I do then?

He clambered to his feet and walked away from me without saying a word.

"Landon."

"What, Rufus?" He swung around to face me. "I'm not what you want, am I? I'm not Stefan. I'm never going to be small and dainty and pretty. So, what can you possibly want from me?"

"Nothing. I don't want anything."

Which was totally the wrong thing to say and not what I meant to come out my mouth at all. Why didn't I think before I spoke? Now Landon was giving me that wide-eyed look like I'd just kicked his puppy, and I knew I'd messed up again. Landon turned his back on me and started up the path that led back to the hotel. I chased after him. Unfortunately, the path was not wide enough for two people to walk side by side, even when one of them wasn't the size of a house.

"Landon, I didn't mean it like that," I called out. He ignored me, forcing me to talk to the broad expanse of his back. "I don't want to be with Stefan, okay? I've been a complete dick this weekend, I know that, but I never meant to hurt you."

"Yet you did it anyway."

"I was an idiot. Last night was a mistake. I had too much to drink and –"

"Are you talking about fucking me or declaring your undying love for Stefan?" Landon threw back over his shoulder.

"Will you please stop and talk to me?"

Landon stopped walking so abruptly I almost collided with him. He spun around and glared at me, folding his arms over his ample chest.

"What, Rufus? What is there left to talk about?"

"Us!" I insisted, craning my neck to look up at him. He stood higher up the path than I did and he was taller than me anyway. Maybe he didn't know it, but he had more than the moral advantage over me at that moment. "I know I've messed up, Landon, but I'm trying here. Just give me one more chance."

Landon closed his eyes and sighed. Then he shook his head. "No."

"No?"

"No more chances, Rufus. Whatever it was between us... it's over. Done."

"You don't mean that."

"I do. I lost my home because of you, Rufus. My parents will probably never talk to me again, also because of you." I opened my mouth to tell him, technically, both of those things were his parents' fault rather than mine, but he cut me off. "You think I'm so desperate for a friend that I'll just accept the way you treat me."

"I'm sorry. I–"

"And, you know what? Before we came here, you might have been right. I actually thought I was falling in love with you, but you know what I realised? You're the desperate one. You don't want me, but you don't want anyone else to have me either."

"I do want you!" I argued vehemently.

"Just not as much as you want Stefan, or anyone else who's cute and sexy and everything I'm not. Admit it, Rufus. Image is everything to you. I don't fit that image and I never will. So... yeah. Let's just leave it, eh?"

He turned and began to climb the path again. I trailed after him. *Talk to him,* they said. *Apologise. Tell him you love him.* Yeah, like I was going to embarrass myself by doing the third when he wouldn't even give me the chance to do the first two. Thing was, he had to care more than he was letting on. Otherwise, why would he be so angry with me? Why was he so determined to put space between us unless he was protecting himself and trying to make sure he didn't get hurt again?

"Go on a date with me," I blurted out as we reached the top of the path. I could see Marcie and Killigan among the guests on the terrace. I couldn't face them until I'd sorted things out with Landon. "One date. That's all."

"Not this again," Landon groaned. "Why can't you just let it go?"

"Because I don't want to," I said. Now that we were on even ground, I walked around him so that I was in front of him and he had to either look at me or turn his back. I got the feeling Landon was too well mannered to do the latter. "One date, Landon. That's all."

"Where?" He didn't exactly sound enthusiastic, but it wasn't a refusal. Maybe there was still hope, after all.

"A concert. Mace White's to be exact." Eric had said not to mention it until he was sure he could get the tickets, but I had to win Landon over somehow and I was not above a bit of bribery.

"I'm not sure." Landon looked at me, big brown eyes filled with doubt. "I've never been to a concert."

I grinned at him, allowing a little of my former cockiness to shine through. "Still not hearing no."

"That's your problem, Rufus," Landon said, stepping around me and heading across the lawns towards the terrace. "I could tell you no until I'm blue in the face. You don't hear it because you don't want to."

"So, is that a yes to the date?"

"It's a maybe," Landon said.

And I swear I heard him chuckle.

CHAPTER 16

THE JOURNEY HOME was a strange one. Although we were booked into the hotel for another night, Killigan announced we were leaving as soon as Stefan and Alex left the reception. Apparently, Landon's, Marcie's and his own luggage were already in the car. We made a brief stop at the hotel to collect my stuff and then we set off. Everyone was tense. Even Marcie and Killigan seemed to be at logger-heads. Marcie was uncharacteristically snappish and Killigan was even more morose and uncommunicative than usual. I hoped it was heading home a day early that had caused their falling out and not me. They'd been good to me. Taken me in when they didn't have to. I didn't want to be the reason they were arguing.

Landon was quiet, staring out of the window at the countryside flashing by. He didn't appear to be angry with me anymore. He just seemed like a man with a lot on his mind. I guess he did. Not only because of me – although he had to still be questioning whether he could trust me or not – but because he didn't know what he was going to find when he got home. He hadn't mentioned his parents at all while we'd been away, so I didn't know if he'd spoken to them. Understandably, he was worried they would have carried through with their threat to kick him out. Part of me wished he would confide in me. Give me some small sign that I was forgiven. But there was another part of me that was glad he didn't because I was rubbish at being empathetic or sympathetic or whatever the hell it was that normal people were when someone they cared about was upset. I wouldn't know what to say and I'd end up letting him down again.

When we pulled up in Landon's driveway, Killigan got out of the car and walked up to the house with him. I watched, slouched in the back seat, as Landon put his key in the lock and turned it. Nothing happened. He tried again with the same result. His bastard parents had changed the locks. Must have done it the second he left the house against their wishes. Landon knocked on the door. Killigan knocked too. He even used the old *open-up-it's-the-police* line, but the Holbys weren't having any of it. There were lights on in the house and a car parked in the driveway, so they were definitely home. Guess they meant it, after all, when they told him not to come back.

Landon and Killigan climbed back into the car. Landon's face was ashen, Killigan's furious. The man might not have had his own kids, and he might have gained a ragtag bunch of sons by accident, but he was fiercely protective when he had to be.

"He's coming back with us," Killigan said gruffly, his tone daring any of us to disagree.

I reached across the car and took Landon's hand, squeezing it lightly. He turned his head to look at me in surprise, but he didn't pull away. Killigan's stern gaze met mine in the rear-view mirror.

"Separate rooms."

"That's okay," Landon answered quietly. "We're not together."

"We're working on it though," I added, although the meaningful look I gave Landon had the opposite effect to the one I intended when he pulled his hand away and went back to staring out of the window.

"It's one date," he muttered.

One date that was still a month away. Even then there were no guarantees. Mason might refuse to give me the tickets. Or maybe Eric hadn't meant it when he made the offer in the first place. Or he'd forget what he'd said the moment he set foot on the plane and the promised tickets would simply never materialise. Worse still, Landon could meet someone else between before we ever got to the concert. Someone who would treat him the way he deserved, not run hot and cold the whole time, so Landon never knew where he stood from one minute to the next.

When we got home, everyone took their overnight bags upstairs to unpack. Killigan showed Landon the spare room and he went inside and closed the door. I emptied my own bag out onto the bed, before shoving everything into either a drawer or the laundry basket. It took me all of five minutes and I felt bad for Landon, because the stuff he had in his bag was the total sum of his belongings at that moment in time. His parents might have kicked him out, but surely they couldn't just keep his stuff? If they tried, I imagined Killigan would come down on them hard. There had to be laws against it.

I toed off my boots and sat on the edge of my bed, indecisive. I wanted to go to Landon and... I don't know... talk to him. Comfort him. Trouble was, I wasn't any good at all that emotional, empathetic shit and Landon knew it. The very real danger was, I'd go in there, mess it up as usual, and end up pushing Landon even further away. I wasn't exactly his favourite person as it was. If he wanted someone to talk to, he'd probably rather it was Killigan or Marnie.

"Fuck it."

I got up and went next door to the spare... or rather Landon's room. The door was still closed, so I tapped on it out of politeness, but then pushed it open without waiting to be invited in. Landon sat on his bed, much in the same position as I had been a few short minutes ago. His bag was on the floor at his feet, unopened.

"Are you okay?"

"No, not really." He didn't look up, so I moved further into the room to stand right in front of him.

"You think it's my fault, don't you? You blame me for them chucking you out."

"Honestly?" Landon tipped his head back to stare at me. I thought he might be crying, but his eyes were dry. He just sat there, looking utterly defeated. Not angry or even particularly sad. Just... like he'd given up. "Out of the two of us, I don't know which of us is most to blame. You? Yeah, definitely, because you asked me to go with you. You made me think we could be more than friends. Let me believe I was starting to mean something to you. Turns out, you only wanted me to go to prove some ridiculous point to Stefan. But you didn't want to be seen with me, did you? Didn't want people to think this fat, tub of lard is the best you can do?"

"It wasn't like that," I muttered. But it was, wasn't it? That was exactly what I'd done, even though I hadn't really intended it to be that way.

"Yes, it was," Landon said flatly. "And that's why I'm as much to blame as you are. Because I knew, deep down, that someone like you would never fancy someone like me, but I chose to believe it. My parents gave me an ultimatum. They told me what would happen if I went away with you, but I *chose* you. It's my own stupid fault. What an idiot, thinking you actually liked me for me."

"I did." I went to sit on the bed beside him. "I *do*. I know I messed up big time, but I promise I wasn't lying when I said I want to be with you. Please, Landon, give me a chance."

"I already am," he grumbled. "I agreed to go to the concert, didn't I? But I swear if you let me down one more time, Rufus..."

"I won't."

"You have to promise."

"No." His eyes widened at that, but at least I was being honest. "I can't promise that I'm never going to hurt you. And you can't promise that you'll never do anything to hurt me. We don't know what could happen tomorrow, or next week or this time next year."

"I seriously doubt I could ever hurt you," Landon scoffed. "You'd have to care about me first."

"I do care about you, idiot." I lightly slapped his meaty thigh, teasingly. "Okay, so what if your parents suddenly decide all is forgiven and you can go home. Would you do it? Even if they made it a condition that you could never have anything to do with me ever again? Because that would hurt me, Landon."

"But why would it?"

"Uh... at the risk of repeating myself... because I like you. And you didn't answer the question. Would you go home if they asked you to?"

I held my breath, waiting for what felt like eternity for him to tell me what I already knew. He wasn't heartless like me and not totally self-absorbed the way I was. His family might not treat him the best, but they were all he knew. If they wanted him home, he would go because he still loved them. There would always be a part of him that wanted to the perfect son he thought they deserved and not the big, fat, gay disappointment he had turned out to be. I didn't want him to leave, but it wouldn't be fair to try and stop him either. Maybe I was struggling – and failing – at being the new and improved Rufus, but I'd let him go if it was what he wanted. The old me would still stamp his feet and cry and sulk, but I'd do my best to keep it behind closed doors for once in my life.

"Actually, I don't know that I would," Landon said finally. "My parents will never accept me for who I am, so maybe it would be stupid to go back and expect anything to have changed. Then again, they're not likely to ask in the first place, so it's kind of pointless even thinking about it."

Without thinking, forgetting this was Landon's room now and he might not want me here, I dropped backwards onto the bed and threw one arm across my eyes. Shit, it wasn't enough that I tried to ruin Eric's life and Stefan and Alex's, or that I'd made such a mess of my own. Now I was buggering up Landon's life as well, without even meaning to. God, I was such a total fuck up.

"No, you're not," Landon said quietly.

I peered out at him from beneath my forearm. "How much of that did I say out loud?"

"Well, I don't know without knowing how much you were thinking." Landon smiled, and I was pleased that I'd unwittingly amused him. "But all you said was that you were a fuck up. And you're not. At least, I don't think you are. Not totally."

"Does that mean you'll give me another chance?" I asked hopefully.

"Maybe." He lowered his bulk down onto the mattress beside me. "But I think we should try being friends first. This concert can be our first official date and then we'll see how it goes. Agreed?"

"Do I have a choice?" I pouted.

"No."

"Fine. Friends until the concert." I poked him in the side and he rolled his head to the side to look at me. "Does that mean no fooling around?"

Landon blinked and then smiled again.

"What did you have in mind?"

CHAPTER 17

THE NEXT FEW weeks passed with surprising speed. Landon settled into the strange family dynamic we had going on with Marcie and Killigan. His parents didn't contact him once, let alone ask him to go home. Landon didn't seem too bothered by the fact his family wanted nothing to do with him. Somehow, Killigan persuaded them to hand over the majority of Landon's belongings, although they refused to give him his laptop as they had paid for it. Landon argued that he'd bought it himself with the money he'd earned at the restaurant, but Killigan told him he had to choose his battles. Whatever that meant.

Both of us returned to our jobs at the restaurant. Alison had employed a new waitress, which meant I got to move into the kitchen and start my journey towards being a chef. To begin with, I was charged with doing the most basic tasks, frying chips and boiling potatoes. It could hardly be called cooking in my book, but during the quieter moments Franco seemed to quite enjoy teaching me how to make some of the restaurant's signature dishes.

It was good in a way that, although he was only in the

dining room next door, Landon and I got a break from each other for a few hours. Living and working together would have been too much for us at a stage when we were still trying to figure out our relationship. Nobody at work had a clue there was anything between us, although Alison obviously knew that Landon was living in the same house after his parents gave him the boot.

It was confusing enough – even for me – to figure out what was happening with Landon. He still maintained that we were friends and not boyfriends, although we were what you might call friends with benefits. He liked me. I knew that much. But Landon drew some sort of moral line at having actual sex, although we were doing pretty much everything else. Enough that Killigan would probably have a blue fit if he knew what we got up to when he and Marcie were fast asleep.

The day of our official first date grew closer. Eric had come through with the tickets as promised, although it worried me slightly that he had arranged backstage passes as well. Mason hated me and wouldn't want me there. I didn't want anything to put a dampener on the evening and Landon was bound to pick up on any negativity coming in my direction. He'd either spoil his night by defending me, or he'd end up questioning his decision to give me another chance.

Thing was, I really had changed recently. I was enjoying working in the restaurant kitchen and enjoying spending time with Landon even more. Okay, so maybe we weren't in a real relationship or publicly dating yet, but I realised that I hadn't given a thought to what other people might say when they saw me with him. The few real friends I had would be pleased that I'd finally found someone who made me happy.

Everyone else could go fuck themselves. If they didn't like me going out with a fat bloke then tough shit. Landon had lost more weight since the wedding, but he was still larger than average. Privately, I thought that, although I wanted him to be healthy, I didn't want him to lose too much weight. Not because I was afraid he'd slim down and decide he could do better than me, but because I'd actually grown rather fond of all his fleshy bits. I liked having something to grab hold of in the heat of passion. Yes, me. The guy who genuinely used to believe fat people would eat him.

"I want to show Landon my romantic side," I said to Killigan a couple of days before the concert. He and I were alone in the house. Marcie had taken Landon out shopping for something nice to wear for our date.

"Okay." Killigan shot me a questioning look. "Why are you telling me?"

"Because I'm not sure I've even got one."

Killigan sighed and reluctantly turned away from the football match he'd been watching on the television.

"And?"

"So, what do I do? What do you do when you want to be romantic with Marcie? I mean you do, don't you? You must do. Don't you?"

"Rufus, I'm not–"

"Please, Killigan. I'm serious." I pressed my palms together like I was praying and fluttered my eyelashes at him. Landon would probably say it was totally sacrilegious to put those two together, but whatever. "You have to help me."

Killigan rolled his eyes and grumbled, but deep inside he was warming to me. I could tell.

"Well, I suppose you could buy him something," he said

eventually. "Marcie likes to be surprised with little presents."

"Okay, like what?"

"Don't ask me." Killigan shrugged. "What sort of thing does he like?"

"I don't know." It was on the tip of my tongue to say blow jobs. Luckily, I managed to restrain myself. Killigan didn't need to know and, besides, I sucked Landon off all the time, so it wouldn't be a *special* present, would it? "What sort of thing do you buy Marcie?"

"Oh, you know... stuff."

I resisted the urge to laugh, because Killigan, the big tough police detective was blushing.

"Oh, my God, Killigan, Do you buy her naughty things?"

"Shut up. And, no, I don't. Marcie likes – and for God's sake, don't tell her I told you this – but she likes pretty underwear."

"Sexy underwear? You mean like crotchless panties and–"

"No!" Killigan leapt to his feet, his face a spectacular shade of red. "I said pretty, as in lace and bows and that sort of thing, not... you know. I really think this conversation is over, Rufus."

He stomped away, although I swear I heard him chuckle to himself out in the hallway. He'd got me thinking though, about what I could buy Landon.

The man in question appeared in the doorway fifteen minutes later, with Marcie close behind him. She looked around the room, puzzled. Football on the TV, which she knew I never watched, and no sign of Killigan. Marcie narrowed her eyes in suspicion.

"What did you do?"

"I think I broke him," I said cheerfully.

"And how did you do that, exactly?"

"I don't know." I gave her my best, wide-eyed innocent look. "All we were doing was talking about your crotchless knickers and–"

Marcie flew from the room and up the stairs like somebody lit a rocket under her backside. Landon shook his head in mock despair, but I thought he was more amused than he was letting on.

"Did you really talk about her... you-know-whats?"

"Hey, don't blame me. Killigan brought it up. I'm an innocent party."

"Yeah, sure you are." He jerked his chin towards the ceiling. "Are you coming up? I'll show you what I bought for the concert."

"Nope. Keep it a surprise." I got to my feet, walking out to the hallway to retrieve my boots from the wooden shoe-rack. "I'm going out. I've got my own shopping to do for Saturday night."

"I thought you said you had too many clothes as it was."

"Who said it was for me?" I stood on tiptoe to plant a kiss on his cheek. "See you later, big guy."

I left the house, happy and smug at the same time. Happy because Landon clearly didn't like me turning him down, which proved he wanted to be with me after all; and smug because I was making a point that he wasn't the one calling all the shots in this... whatever it was between us. If he was so insistent that he wasn't my boyfriend, then he had no right to act like one when it suited him to do so.

I wasn't out long. I'd known exactly where I was going and the lady in the shop was nice enough to help me find what I was looking for. When I got home, precious package hidden in my jacket, Killigan and Landon were sat at the dining room table. Marcie was about to serve dinner.

"Sit," she said.

"It's okay, I'll get something later at the restaurant."

"You'll eat now," she snapped, fixing me with an icy stare. "Now, sit down."

"Can I just–"

"Sit, Rufus!"

I slunk into the nearest chair before I got shouted at again, then yelped when Killigan kicked me under the table.

"She's still mad as Hell over the knickers thing," he hissed and kicked me again for good measure. "This is all your fucking fault, dickwad."

"Ow! That hurt." I reached down to massage my shin and scowled at him across the table. "How fucking old are you, anyway, shithead?"

"Rufus!" Somehow, Marcie managed to hear what I said and not Killigan. She smacked me smartly around the back of the head and Killigan smirked. "I won't have bad language at the table. Now, please... can we just have a nice family meal together, without any drama or complaining or smutty talk."

She took her place at the table and we all began to pick at our food. Problem was, from my point of view, if I wasn't being dramatic, bitchy or smutty, I didn't seem to have an awful lot to say. I had to settle for shooting Killigan sullen looks across the table. To be fair, he gave back as good as he got. Landon was quiet, which was nothing new, but then he hadn't been with us long enough to see Marcie in a bad mood yet. Knowing Landon, he would be worried it was because of him and he'd be waiting for the insults to start flying in his direction. I hated seeing him retreat into to himself, when he'd come so far in recent weeks.

"So, Rufus, did you buy anything nice while you were out?" Marcie asked, her voice a little too loud, her smile forced and tight. She was trying though, I had to give her that.

"Actually, I did," I said, subconsciously putting my hand over the package hidden inside my jacket. Thankfully, Marcie hadn't insisted I take the jacket off before I sat down, otherwise it would have spoiled Landon's surprise for later. "But it's a present for Landon so..."

"For me?" Landon looked up in surprise, although who did he think I meant when I told him earlier that I wasn't shopping for myself? "Really?"

"No, not really. I bought something for the other bloke I'm taking to an Arcadia concert on Saturday night."

Landon's face fell. He blinked and looked at me doubtfully. Killigan tutted and shook his head.

"He's joking. Of course it's for you."

"Well, what is it?" Landon asked curiously. "Can I see it?"

Christ, you'd think nobody had ever bought him anything before.

"No, not yet. It's a surprise. You can have it when we get home from work."

"No hanky-panky!" Killigan said.

Landon and I looked at each other and burst out laughing.

CHAPTER 18

THE RESTAURANT WAS full that night, with two large parties in. I hardly got to see Landon at all, but even at our busiest in the kitchen, the promise of presenting him with his gift when we got home was never far from my mind. He would love it, I was sure. Finally, I seemed to be getting something right when it came to this romancing business. I was going to prove to Landon I could be caring and considerate and he'd be so appreciative of my efforts, he'd be putty in my hands.

After the restaurant closed, we hurried home. Landon didn't mention the present, but I knew he was just as excited about it as I was. I got the impression his parents had not given him much in the way of presents outside of birthdays and Christmas. And I knew he'd never had a boyfriend before me to shower him with any impromptu romantic gifts.

Marcie and Killigan were already in bed when we got back to the house. We knew they were asleep because Killigan's loud snores reverberated along the landing. I ducked into my room to collect Landon's present from where I'd hidden it earlier and then scuttled along the landing to where Landon was waiting, sitting on the side of the bed, in his own room.

I dropped the package into his lap, grinning like an idiot. Because this was the start of something, I could feel it in my bones. After this, Landon wouldn't be able to deny anymore that we were meant to be together.

"What is it?" He turned the square of tissue paper – purple, naturally – over in his hands.

"Open it and see."

Carefully, he peeled back the paper and I waited with baited breath. Landon's jaw dropped open as he held the purple lace material up between his thumb and forefinger. I bounced on the balls of my feet with my excitement, my brain not fully registering yet that he didn't seem as enamoured by my gift as I thought he would be.

"Is this a joke?" Landon asked faintly, his gaze still firmly locked on the beautiful pair of lace panties I'd given him. Extra large, naturally, but they could still be considered flimsy and sexy.

"What? No." A small amount of my enthusiasm fizzled out of existence, quashed by the weight of his inexplicable negativity. "I thought you could wear them to the concert."

"Are you serious?" Landon asked. He dropped the panties back into the wrapping paper, screwed the whole thing into a ball, and thrust it back at me. I didn't take it and he tossed it onto the bed with a disgusted look on his face. "You really expect me to go to a rock concert wearing a pair of women's knickers?"

"Well, no... not if you don't want to." I was beginning to feel like I'd done something wrong, although it was impossible to figure out what. Didn't everyone like to receive sexy underwear as a gift? I'd even made sure to listen to Killigan and buy something pretty as opposed to overtly sexual. I wanted Landon to feel good about himself and I thought I was being nice. Obviously, Landon saw it differently, though I failed to understand why. "I thought you'd look sexy in them. That's all."

"Sexy?" Landon's voice went up an octave and he laughed bitterly. "I wouldn't look sexy, Rufus. I'd look ridiculous. And I'd feel it too. What possessed you to think I'd ever want something like that? God, if my parents ever found out..."

"Don't show them then!" I fired back, suddenly furious.

I mean, really? I'd gone out especially, spent my hard-earned money on buying him a present, something special and romantic and he was just going to throw it back in my face like I'd offended him? Well, he was the one who'd offended me by rejecting my gift and making me out to be the bad guy in all this.

"You're unbelievable!" Landon yelled, uncharacteristically loud and angry. "You'll never change, Rufus. You're as bad as all the others and I should never have trusted you. All you want to do is make me look stupid."

"I was being nice!"

"What? So, you can tell your ex and his famous boyfriend that I like wearing women's underwear? Is that the plan? Then you all have a bloody good laugh at me, is that it?"

The bedroom door flew back on its hinges and Killigan stormed into the room, dressed only in a pair of saggy grey boxer shorts. Marcie came in behind him, more discreetly attired in a flannel robe.

"What the Hell is going on in here?" Killigan demanded, hands on hips and oblivious as to how totally un-intimidating he was at that precise moment.

"It's him!" Both Landon and I yelled at the same time, pointing accusing fingers at each other.

Naturally, they both took Landon's side. Marcie went to sit on the bed beside him and put her arm around his shoulders, while Killigan glared at me, automatically assuming it was my fault.

"He got me these," Landon said, grabbing the puddle of purple lace from the wrapping paper and holding them up for Killigan to see. "This is my so-called present."

"How many times?" I cried, exasperated. "I. Was. Being. *Nice.*"

"Sweetheart, are you sure?" Marcie asked, rubbing Landon's back like he was a baby. Then again, he was acting like a big baby, so if the cap fit... "If the intention was to be nice, I'm not sure you would have bought something so... so..."

"Insulting, that's what those are," Killigan ground out. "You're taking the piss out of him, aren't you? I should have known you were setting him up, you nasty little–"

I didn't hang around to hear the end of that sentence. There was no need. I already knew what Killigan thought of me. What he'd *always* thought of me. I ran back to my bedroom, slamming the door behind me and throwing myself onto the bed. It was so unfair. Why should I take all the blame just because Landon had over-reacted to a pair of stupid panties? How come nobody even noticed the panties were purple? They all knew how much I loved purple. If I gave something purple as a gift, then it should prove how serious I was being. I'd never make a joke of it.

A few moments later there was a knock on the door. I buried my face in the pillow and responded with a muffled "Go away."

But, because it was Killigan and he was an arsehole, and

because it was his house more than it was mine, he ignored me and came in anyway. I didn't even have to lift my head to see it was him. I could hear him huffing and puffing in the doorway. If I did look up, I bet I'd see him all puffed up, displaying like an alpha-male chimpanzee.

"You mind telling me what that was all about?" Killigan demanded gruffly. "After I specifically told you not to do anything to hurt that boy?"

"What about me?" I sat up, trying to brush away the tears before Killigan saw I was crying, but the damn things leaked from my eyes faster than I could wipe. "I'm hurt too."

"Right. And how are you hurt exactly, Rufus? Tell me that. Did Landon trick you into believing he'd bought you something nice? Does he build you up, only to tear you down every chance that he gets? Does he humiliate you, time and time again, in front of your friends? Did he fuck you and then tell you he was in love with somebody else? Come on. What did Landon do to injure your oh-so-sensitive feelings, Rufus?"

"He... he... he didn't like my present!" I wailed, sobbing in earnest now.

Killigan wouldn't understand. He'd think I was faking it. Turning on the waterworks to get myself out of trouble, the way he'd probably been told I always did. By Eric, Alex. Probably even Stefan. And, before, it might have been true. But before, it hadn't hurt this bad. Before, I hadn't cared this much.

"You're serious." Killigan sounded surprised. But he also sounded as though he might actually believe me. Maybe I was kidding myself, but I thought he seemed less angry than he had when he'd burst into my room without knocking. Okay, so he did knock, but I didn't say he could enter, did I? Just the oppo-site, in fact. He sighed heavily and came to sit on the bed beside me. "Okay, let's try this again, shall we? Calmly this time. Why the fu... why would you give Landon something like that? Were you taking the piss, or did you really expect him to like them?"

"I thought he'd... like them..." I hiccupped, still dabbing at the stupid bloody tears that refused to stop.

"Why though? Has he ever expressed an interest in women's underwear? Did he say something to suggest he'd like to try it? Help me out here, Rufus. I really want to understand."

"They're pretty," I sniffed. "Like you said."

"Like I...? Jesus, Rufus. Don't tell me you bought Landon knickers because of what I said."

"But they're purple," I said. "And... did I mention that they're pretty?"

"Yes, but..." Killigan shook his head and ran a hand over his face tiredly. "Rufus, have you considered that you bought what you bought because *you* like purple ladies' knickers rather than getting something that Landon would like?"

"I don't know. Maybe." I didn't think I'd done that, although I was obsessed with the colour purple, of course. It certainly hadn't been my intention though. If I *had* gone out and bought something for Landon that was really more for me, then I had to be even more selfish than I realized. "I mean, I like them, yes. I thought they were pretty and the felt nice, but that's why I wanted Landon to have them. I don't blame you for not believing me, Killigan, but I just wanted Landon to feel good about himself. I thought if he wore them, he'd feel nice and sexy and maybe it would even boost his confidence a bit. I wanted him to know I see him as an attractive, sensual man and not just some big fat jelly-belly."

"Shit, Rufus..." Killigan stared at me, although not unkindly. "Couldn't you have just told him that instead of embarrassing the poor lad?"

"Yeah, well... it's a bit late now," I muttered ruefully. "He's never going to listen to me."

"You should give it a go. You're always asking him for another chance, aren't you? Maybe it's time you gave him one?"

"I can try." I wiped my eyes again, thankful that the blubbing seemed to be under control at least. "I'll go and talk to him."

"You don't have to," Landon said from the doorway. "I heard everything."

CHAPTER 19

I WOULDN'T SAY things went back to normal after what Killigan laughingly referred to as Knickergate – although, thankfully, not in front of Landon or Marcie – but nobody seemed to hold what had happened against me. In fact, there seemed to be an unspoken agreement that the whole event, Killigan's teasing aside, was not to be mentioned again. The offending underwear vanished, which was slightly annoying because I could at least have tried to get my money back. The damn things hadn't been cheap, but I didn't dare ask where they had disappeared to.

Finally, the day of the concert rolled around. Landon looked nice in a new pair of faded denim jeans and a black button-down shirt. I had on white jeans, while everything else from my hair to my boots to my glittering eyeshadow and nail varnish were varying shades of purple. Marcie insisted on taking a photograph of the two of us before we left the house, like we were going on a prom date or something.

Mason sent a car for us, early enough that we could meet the band and hang out with everyone before the show.

I knew it was more for Landon's benefit than mine, but I wasn't offended. These guys knew it was his first ever concert and they wanted to make it a memorable experience for him. That was what I wanted too, so I guess – for the first time in my life – I had to swallow my pride and let my date be the centre of attention. I could do it. I could act like a grown up for one whole night and give Landon the best date ever. All I had to do then, was hope Landon didn't end up liking one of them more than he liked me.

When we arrived at the venue, we were met by a minion and given lanyards with laminated passes that granted us access via the artists' entrance. Then we were escorted down long, white-washed corridors and into a green room that was bigger than both mine and Landon's bedrooms combined. The band were scattered around the plush sofas and chairs in various states of repose. Eric, who was sat on Mason's lap, jumped up and came over to give me an awkward hug.

"Let me introduce you to everyone," Eric said, like everybody else in the room was not incredibly famous and we didn't know who they were already. "Mason, you've met, of course."

"It's Mace," Mason grumbled. "Technically, I'm working."

"Sorry, babe. So, Mace..." Eric pointed to each person as he said their name. "Donovan. Heath. Crash and that's Dixie. Guys, this is my... um... friend, Rufus."

"Rufus is his ex," Mason pointed out helpfully. Eric narrowed his eyes at him and Mason dropped his gaze. I wondered why he was being such a dick. If he really objected that strongly to my presence, he could have just said no to giving me the tickets in the first place.

"Ah, the infamous ex." Donovan gave me an appraising

look from his slouched position on one of the sofas. "I've heard a lot about you. We all have."

"And I bet none of it was good."

"Nope. Not a word of it." Donovan grinned at me and I couldn't help but smile back.

I mean, yes, I was on a date, but the guy was still seriously hot with his shaggy black hair and ivory skin. He wasn't built like a brick shithouse either, which was much more to my taste than the over-the-top muscular build of Mason. Although, it was funny, despite Donovan's good looks and the fact I probably wouldn't stand a chance with him anyway, I didn't even want to try to get in his pants. I wouldn't do that to Landon. Shit, maybe I had really changed. We weren't even in a proper relationship yet and there was basically no material gain to be had from being with Landon, but I didn't want cheat on him. I didn't want to hurt him. Which made me feel bad for Eric in a way, because I'd been unfaithful to him countless times when we were living together and I'd never cared in the slightest how he would feel if he found out.

"This is Landon," I said, grabbing Landon's hand and pulling him closer to me. "And he's a concert virgin, so promise you'll be gentle with him."

To my surprise, Mason was the first one to laugh.

"Well, shit. Guess the bitch has a heart after all."

"Mason!" Eric reprimanded sharply.

"It's fine," I said quickly, because the last thing I wanted was to cause a scene between my ex and his new love right before that new love was due to go on stage. "I mean, he's not wrong, is he? I am a bitch."

I pursed my glossy lips and fluttered my eyelashes and the ice was broken. Everyone relaxed. Eric went back to sit on Mason's lap and the big guy immediately wrapped his arms around his waist, anchoring him in place. Landon and I settled, side by side, on the sofa between Dixie and Heath. Donovan stretched out on his own sofa and closed his eyes, although it was obvious to me that he was not asleep. Crash, the band's aptly named drummer, paced the room, playing imaginary beats on thin air.

"Love the eyeshadow, by the way," Eric said lightly. He wasn't into dressing up and make-up the way Stefan and I were, but he'd never had any objection to seeing me wear it. "And the nails too. You always did love that sparkly shit."

"Yeah." I held up my hand and waggled my fingers at him. "This glitter stuff is a bitch to get off though."

"Soak your nails in a bowl of remover for a couple of minutes before you try and take it off," Mason suggested, straight-faced. "That usually does the trick."

Everybody turned to stare at him. Even Donovan opened one eye and smirked.

"And here I was thinking you were nothing more than a musclebound idiot who could sing a bit," I said dryly.

"Hey, these muscles are honestly come by," Mason objected, amid the others laughter. "I work hard to keep this body. If you want to see muscles that come from years of steroid abuse, I'll introduce you to our roadie, Ray. See if you can tell the difference."

"Oh, my God, tell them what he does!"

Eric bounced up and down excitedly on Mason's lap and the others laughed, obviously already aware of what Eric was referring to.

"Okay, so this guy, Ray, he never takes a shit," Mason chuckled. "And he never finishes when he has sex, if you know what I mean. It's true, I swear. He thinks if he comes, it will detract from his body mass."

"Does that really work?" Landon asked innocently.

"Because if ejaculating is a certified way of losing weight, I'll be wanking every hour on the hour."

We all fell about laughing again, making Landon blush. I squeezed his hand and smiled at him.

"For the record, I like you the way you are, but if you decide that cum is going to be your chosen weight loss program, then you don't need to waste it on wanking. Just saying."

"What if it works both ways and his cum makes you fat though?" Eric asked thoughtfully.

"It won't," I assured him. "I promise you, there'll be just as much coming out as there is going in."

"Ewww! And that's enough of that conversation," Heath said in a panicked tone, looking at Landon and I as if he was worried we were going to set about proving it there and then on the same sofa as him. "Can we please talk about something else?"

"Heath is married," Donovan explained, without bothering to open his eyes. "To a woman. He doesn't like sex talk for the simple reason he's not getting any."

"Screw you," Heath replied with no real animosity.

"Fine by me, bro, if it releases some of that sexual tension you got going on."

And that was the way it carried on for the next couple of hours. A lot of banter and teasing and laughing. Best of all, everyone seemed to forget that Landon and I were strangers and didn't really belong in that room. With the rich and famous. They included us and treated us exactly the same as they treated each other. We felt like we were part of the gang, even if it was for one night only and by morning we'd be back to being the apprentice chef and the waiter who may or may not be boyfriends.

Eventually, the band had to get ready to go on stage.

Landon and I were given the choice of watching from the wings or taking the seats Eric had reserved for us in the auditorium. Apparently, Mason and the other guys hated playing to seated venues because they said it impacted the way the audience responded to them. The venue we were at was a compromise. The arena floor was standing only, with raised seating around the sides. Because it was Landon's first show and I was a short-arse who would get swamped by the crowd, Eric had decided to book us seats. And because I wanted Landon to experience the show as a fan and not a guest of the band, we opted to take the seats, which were close to the stage on the right-hand side.

"Hey, good view," Landon said happily as we sat.

"Well, it was." A shrill voice came from behind us. "It's bloody typical. Every single time, the biggest, fattest person in the whole place has to sit in front of me."

The joy drained from Landon's face and he dropped his head, cheeks flaming with shame and embarrassment. I swivelled around in my seat to glare at the couple sat behind us. The woman, stick thin and with a pinched face, glared back. It looked like she was a bigger bitch than me and that was saying something.

"For your information," I said coldly. "He paid for his seat exactly the same as you." Not that he had of course, but she didn't know that. "And if you don't want anyone sitting in front of your scraggy arse, then buy your tickets earlier and get the front row. Otherwise, keep your worthless, idiotic opinions to yourself."

The woman gawped at me for a moment and then turned to her male companion with an expectant look.

"Are you going to let him talk to me like that?"

"Oh, it's a him, is it?" the bloke answered with a sneer.

"I was wondering. Only it's hard to tell with all that make-up. I reckon it wishes it was a woman."

Landon spun around his seat, surprisingly fast given his bulk, before I could even think of a suitably scathing retort to the guy's attack on my masculinity. I'd never seen Landon look as angry as he did at that moment and I actually grabbed his arm, fearful he might actually try punching the guy. Not that the prick didn't deserve it, but I didn't have Landon pegged as a fighter and I didn't want him getting hurt. I also didn't want us to get thrown out before the band were even on stage.

"For your information," Landon spat, echoing my words from a moment ago. "He is most definitely a *him*. He has a dick and, I assure you, he knows what to do with it. I bet I'm a lot more satisfied than your missus is."

"What the fuck...?"

The guy leapt to his feet. He was taller than me, but no match for Landon's height and build. Luckily, the guy didn't know that Landon had never thrown a punch in his life. Landon stood and the guy backed down instantly. He paled slightly and quickly looked around, I thought at first, to make sure nobody else had witnessed the exchange. But then he said:

"I'll call security and get you thrown out."

"Don't bother. We're going." I smiled at him sweetly and took Landon's hand. "Come on, lover-boy. Let's go and watch from the wings like Mace said we could."

The couple looked at each other and then their jaws dropped open with such perfect synchronicity it was comical. I sent Eric a quick text to let him know we were heading back and then, laughing, Landon and I hurried back through the packed hallways to the door we'd exited just a short while before. Security saw our passes and opened the door for us. Eric waited on the other side and quickly pulled us inside.

"What's going on?" he asked. "How come you changed your mind?"

"Landon started a fight," I said gleefully.

"Seriously?"

"It's true. He was defending my honour."

"You defended mine first," Landon said, smiling again.

Eric shook his head in disbelief, but I could see the amusement in his eyes.

"I never could take you anywhere, Rufus," he teased. "Now, it looks like you're being a bad influence on young Landon."

"Hey, what makes you so sure he's not being one on me?"

"Because I know you too well, Rufus." He raised his eyebrows at me, but I could tell he was only messing around. "Anyway, we should get a move on. They're going on stage any minute."

Landon went all eager-beaver on me and practically ran down the corridor to the backstage area. Chuckling, I went to follow him, but Eric stopped me. I gave him a confused look, wondering why he would call me back when he'd just said we had to hurry.

"I've never seen you like this before," he said. "You really like this guy, don't you?"

"I really do. I've never felt like this about anyone in my whole life." I blushed, suddenly remembering I was talking to the man with whom I shared my bed and my home. "Sorry. I didn't say that to be a bitch, Eric."

"It's okay," Eric said with a wry smile. "I always knew you didn't really love me, but there's no hard feelings. Look at us now. I'm the happiest I've ever been now I'm with

Mason and you're all loved up with Landon. I think we're exactly where we're meant to be, Rufus, and who we're meant to be with."

"So long as I don't fuck it up again," I told him, puzzled when a worried look crossed his face.

"I need to talk to Donovan," he said, before dashing away at high speed.

Whatever he had to so urgently tell the guitarist would have to wait though. The crowd roared and the first heavy notes of Arcadia's intro reverberated around the building. The show had begun.

CHAPTER 20

"BEST NIGHT EVER!" I yelled, barely able to keep myself from bouncing up and down in excitement.

The final notes of the encore faded and the band ran off stage, all of them dripping with sweat. Donovan noticed me standing there and grinned. He shook his head, showering me with droplets of perspiration. I squealed and ducked behind Landon for protection. Not that it was a great improvement. Landon was red in the face and probably just as sweaty as the band. He'd thoroughly enjoyed watching the show from the wings and danced the whole night long. I'd enjoyed watching him almost as much as watching the band. He danced with wild abandonment and without fear of being ridiculed. Everyone backstage was either too busy working or watching the show to give a toss about the fat bloke jiggling away to the music. Landon turned to face me, his face aglow with happiness.

"Okay, as first dates go, that was pretty epic," he said. "Don't know how you're going to top that on our second."

"There's going to be a second then?"

"Hope so."

He smiled, before following one of the crew back to the green room where the band would meet us once they had showered and changed. I glanced at Eric, who still wore that concerned expression. He didn't seem to enjoy his boyfriend's show at all. During the interval, I'd seen him try more than once, to get Donovan on his own. With each failed attempt, Eric's mood seemed to worsen. He'd sounded genuine when he said he was happy with Mason. Maybe it was a case of the pot calling the kettle black, but I really hoped Eric wasn't messing around with Donovan behind Mason's back.

It didn't take long for the guys to wander back into the green room, looking and smelling a good deal fresher than they had when they'd come off stage. One of the crew even loaned Landon a clean shirt and a splash of deodorant when they saw he had sweated through the one he had been wearing.

Mason strolled into the room, dropped into a chair and pulled Eric into his lap without hesitation. Eric's gaze went to Donovan, but the guitarist didn't even spare him a glance. If there was something going on between them, Donovan was doing a better job of hiding it than Eric.

"After show party anybody?" Donovan called out. "I hired a suite at the Hilton." I wasn't sure he was including Landon and I in the invitation. We'd already pushed our luck that night; free tickets to a sold-out show, hanging out with the band, watching from the side of the stage. I'd given Landon the perfect first date with the help of the guys and I really couldn't expect anything else from them. Then Donovan looked directly at me, a challenge in his bold stare. "Are you guys in?"

"You don't have to," Eric said quickly. "You can just call it a night and go home if you like. I'll call for a car."

. . .

"What the hell, Eric?" Mason looked at him surprise. "You're the one who wanted them here."

"Yeah, I do. It's just... you know, I thought Landon might be tired or something."

"I'm fine," Landon said cheerfully, apparently oblivious to the underlying tension in the room. "And I'd love to go to a party. I'm having a good time and I'm not ready for it to end yet."

"Well said, my man." Donovan threw an arm around Landon's shoulders and then winked at me. I frowned back, unable to shake the feeling that I was missing something. "Let's go. Last man standing pays the bar bill."

We all trailed out of the green room. The venue had underground parking for the performing artists, which was secure and kept them out of sight of any over-zealous fans who might be hanging around, waiting for them to leave. Even so, the band members were escorted to the waiting line of town cars by security, although given none of them matched Mason in size, I questioned whether he needed an escort in the first place.

Ahead of me, Landon climbed into one of the cars with Crash and Dixie. Suddenly, Donovan grabbed my arm and pulled me towards the next car in line.

"We'll take this one. There's more room." He gave me a leering look. "And it'll be more private, if you know what I mean."

Okay, I didn't like where this was going. I'd suspected he had something going on with Eric and now he was hitting on me? Was that why Eric didn't want me to go to the party? Was he jealous because he knew his bit on the side was interested in someone else? Well, I could soon put him right on that score. Landon was right fucking there, for God's sake. I wasn't going to cheat on him while we were on a date. Even I wouldn't sink that low, which again, was testament to how much I'd changed recently, because before I wouldn't have hesitated before leaping into bed with hot, rich guy and sod the boyfriend.

"Eric! Mason! Come in this one," I called out quickly, just as they were about to duck into the third car.

Mason hesitated and seemed like he was about to refuse, but Eric looked relieved and grabbed his boyfriend's arm, tugging him over to join us. Wow. Life among the rich and famous had certainly changed my sweet-natured, naïve ex-partner and not for the better. He had no shame, flaunting his jealousy over Donovan in front of the man who was supposed to be the love of his life. I couldn't believe Mason was blind to what was going on.

The ride to the hotel was strained, all of us having a personal reason for being on edge. Thankfully, it was late at night and traffic was light, so it took us less than twenty minutes to arrive. By the sound of things, when the elevator doors opened at the penthouse on the top floor, the party had already started.

I spotted Landon straight away, sat on a sofa by himself and looking decidedly uncomfortable. He glanced up in obvious relief when I called his name. Bounding across the room, I landed in his lap, seizing his mouth in a searing kiss. Maybe I was being childish and trying to prove a point to anyone watching. Maybe I just wanted to kiss my boyfriend. When we broke apart, he grinned self-consciously.

"People are looking, Rufus."

"Let them," I declared. "They're only jealous."

"Of what?"

"Of me." I kissed him again. "Because you're mine and they can't have you."

"Rufus, don't..." Landon dropped his gaze and shook his head. He thought I was teasing him again. That I didn't really want him and nor would anyone else in the room. "Why are you even bothering with me? Donovan has made it pretty clear that..."

"That he's an arrogant prick?" I finished for him. "Yeah, he is, but I don't care about Donovan. This is our first official date, remember? You're not getting rid of me that easily, big guy."

"Do you mind?" Landon asked quietly. His gaze flickered to where Donovan was holding court in the corner of the room. "That I'm still so big, I mean? I wouldn't blame you for going with him if you wanted to. He's a lot better looking than I am."

"Meh. He's okay if you like that sort of thing. As for you..." I swivelled in his lap so that I straddled his thighs and put both hands on his stomach. "This is part of you. I wouldn't have asked you out on a date if I minded, would I? Actually, I kind of like your belly, so lose weight if it means you'll be healthier, Landon, but don't do it on my account."

He hugged me tightly, squishing me against his chest. Laughing, I pushed myself upright.

"So, now that's sorted, who do I have to suck to get a drink around here?"

"Me!" Landon dumped me off of his lap and onto the sofa cushion and was on his feet in the blink of an eye. "Nobody but me. Well, later... obviously. Not right now."

"I suppose I can wait if you can, big guy."

His eyes widened slightly, like he wasn't sure if I was joking or not. Then he turned on his heel and went in search of some liquid refreshment.

A few drinks later and I was ready to get down on my knees and blow Landon there and then, never mind the audience. My man seemed to have something against mixers of any kind and each drink he fetched me was a little stronger than the last.

"I need a piss."

I leaned over Landon who – for some strange reason given we were at a party – was deep in conversation with Heath over some book they'd both read and thought very highly of. Heath lifted a hand and gestured vaguely to a door on the other side of the room. Leaving them to their discussion, that was so intellectual it went way over my head, I swayed across the room and through the door Heath had indicated. My jaw hit the floor at the marble and gold-leaf bathroom that was probably the most over-the-top, ostentatious room I'd ever seen. It made a man ashamed of sullying perfection by urinating into the gleaming porcelain bowl.

Still, if you gotta go, then you gotta go. I did what I needed to do and went to the sink to wash my hands. The liquid soap that splashed into my palm from a golden dispenser smelt divine. I resolved to find out what it was before we left, in the hopes Marcie could be persuaded to deviate from the horrible lavender stuff she favoured.

I opened the door to go back to the party and see if Landon had finished being boring yet and came face to face with Donovan. Well... face to neck. Like most men, he was a good deal taller than me. Donovan put his hands on my shoulders and pushed me back into the bathroom. He closed and locked the door behind him, then leaned on it for good measure. You know, just to make sure I *really* had no chance of escape.

"You're cute, you know that? Downright hot, in fact."

"Um... yeah... thanks." I took a step backwards, putting distance between us. Mentally, I crossed my fingers and hoped that Landon hadn't seen him come in here.

"So, what are you doing with old blubber-guts out there?" he asked, jerking a thumb over his shoulder.

"I'm sorry, what did you just say?"

"Come on, you must see it. You're wasted on a guy like that. You deserve better than some big, jelly-belly bouncing around on top of you." He eyed me up and down. "I mean, I'm assuming you're the bottom. Let's face it, you'd probably lose your dick in that fat arse. Any man would. Even me and... trust me... my dick is huge. Big enough to satisfy a little sweetheart like you, that's for sure."

"Hold on a minute," I ground out furiously, deciding it would be best to ignore the comment about his dick, seeing as I couldn't think of an appropriate answer. "Who the fuck do you think you are, talking about Landon like that?"

"I think I'm the rich famous guy with a body to die for, who's going to save you from Mr. Zero-Personality, before he rolls over in the night and squashes you flat," Donovan said confidently.

"Fuck you!"

"Well, yeah, that's kinda what I was hoping..."

"Sorry, what I meant to say was... *fuck you!*" I spat. The guy was unbelievable. Okay, the old me would have been all over him like a rash and fucked him senseless in a heartbeat. But I wasn't the old me. I was the new and improved me and I had a boyfriend. "You might be famous and have money and a nice body, but you're a cunt."

"Whoa! Easy there, tiger." Donovan held up his hands defensively, but I knew he was laughing at me.

"Landon is worth ten of you."

"Hey, it's your choice..."

"Damn right it is. And I'd choose Landon over you every single day for the rest of my fucking life," I told him angrily. "I love him. Yeah, you heard me. I love him, jelly-belly and all, so you can fuck right off."

"Oh, alright, calm your tits, Sparkles," Donovan said, his expression turning serious. "I'm just messing with you. It was a test and you passed, okay?"

"What test? What are you on about?" I stared at him in bewilderment. I thought I'd sobered up when he first pushed me back into the bathroom, but now I wondered if I was still blind drunk, because what his words made no sense whatsoever.

"Mace and Eric," he explained, totally unrepentant. "They asked me to hit on you and see how fast you dumped your fat boyfriend."

"They did what?" Suddenly, I was stone cold sober. And I believed him. This whole thing had been a test from the start. Eric had set me up to fail. I could understand why he'd want to get back at me for the way I'd acted in the past, but why do something that would deliberately hurt Landon? I thought back to Eric's strange behaviour earlier and realized it had only started after I'd told him how much Landon meant to me. That's why he had been so desperate to speak to Donovan. He'd tried to stop the plan to seduce me from going ahead. "You're not messing about with Eric behind Mason's back, are you?"

"What the hell...? No, of course not. Like Eric would ever look twice at anyone else. Plus, Mason would kill me."

Right. So, Saint Eric wouldn't cheat, but I would? In Eric's experience not only would I, but I had. Over and over again. I guess I couldn't blame him for assuming I would do it to Landon too, but I was so damn angry. What-ever had happened between us in the past, he had no right to try and force me into a situation where I'd cheat on Landon.

"Would you mind moving out of my way?" I said stiffly. "I have to find my boyfriend and get the fuck out of here."

Donovan nodded and stood aside to let me leave. I threw open the door and pushed through the crowd to where I'd left Landon. Heath was nowhere to be seen and a guilty-looking Eric had taken his place.

"I'm so sorry, Rufus," Eric said. "I tried to tell him not to."

"Not to what?" Landon looked between us, confused. "What is he talking about, Rufus?"

"It's nothing," I answered, blanking Eric. "Come on. We're going."

"Why?"

Despite his question, Landon didn't argue. He got to his feet and followed me into the elevator. I didn't bother saying goodbye to anyone. These people were not my friends. They could rot in hell as far as I was concerned.

"Rufus, wait. At least let me get you a car." Eric chased after us, but I pressed the button for the ground floor and the doors closed in his face before he could say anything else.

"What's going on?" Landon asked worriedly, as the elevator descended.

"I'll tell you," I promised. "Later though. It's just something stupid, Landon. I don't want it to spoil tonight."

"Fine," Landon grumbled. "But seeing you upset has already ruined it for me."

"I'm okay. More angry than upset." We left the hotel and looked up and down the street. "Now all we need to do is find a bloody taxi."

CHAPTER 21

DESPITE THE TIME OF NIGHT – or more accurately, the time of morning – or perhaps because of it, we found a cab with no trouble at all. Landon had reservations about getting in when the cab pulled into the kerb, muttering some nonsense about whether the driver was kosher or not. The car had a taxi sign on the top, but no obvious sign of a meter. But I was tired and pissed off and I wanted to go home and forget all about Eric and Mason setting me up the way they had. Plus, I had to admit – even if only to myself – that I was just a little bit pissed off that Donovan had only come onto me because Eric had told him to. He hadn't really fancied me at all. Not that I wanted him to. I'd blown him off even before finding out he wasn't genuine, but yeah... my ego was still a little bruised.

"Just get in," I said shortly.

We got into the back of the car and Landon wrinkled his nose.

"Rufus, this is a bad idea. The whole car stinks of booze."

"So do we." I shrugged. "I expect it was his last passengers. Stop worrying will you."

Landon gave me a hurt look. I was sorry for snapping at him, but I'd really had enough of being Nice Rufus for one night. The old me was far more likely to assert himself when I was feeling so irritable and exhausted.

"I was saving this for when we got home," Landon whispered, darting a glance at the driver. "But if it cheers you up, I'll tell you now."

"Tell me what? You can't be pregnant. We haven't done it since the wedding. Besides, how would we tell?"

Landon stared at me for a moment, as if he was trying to decide if I was joking or not. He leaned back in his seat and folded his arms.

"You don't have to be a bitch, Rufus."

"Sorry." I nudged him with my elbow. "So, go on... what were you going to tell me?"

"No," he said stubbornly. "I don't think you deserve to know now."

"Please?" I snuggled up to him and fluttered my eyelashes. He shook his head, but I thought I caught a glimpse of a smile. "Come on, Landon. What is it?"

"It's a surprise," he muttered.

"I love surprises! So long as it's better than the one I gave you, of course."

"Actually, it's the same one."

I narrowed my eyes at him. "You bought me underwear?"

"No, you bought me underwear." He glanced at the driver again. He lowered his voice. "I just happen to be wearing it. That's your surprise."

"Oh my God!" I squealed. "Show me!"

"What? Not here. Rufus, what are you doing?" Landon

giggled and tried to pull away from me as I lunged at him, grabbing at the hem of his shirt. "Rufus, stop! Okay, just a peek. Then you'll have to wait until we get home."

He lifted the hem of his borrowed shirt and pulled the waistband of his jeans down, barely an inch. Even in the dim light I could see the purple lace. I couldn't stop the smile that spread across my face until my jaw ached. He'd kept the panties and he'd worn them on our date. And the little minx had had them on all night and not even hinted at the fact. My man had a naughty side and I liked it.

Landon gasped as I slipped a finger into his waistband and rubbed it against the soft material. He looked at me, his pupils lust-blown, and I smiled. Oh, I was getting laid tonight. Better hope Killigan had his ear-lugs in because I intended to get loud.

"God, I love you," I breathed, my finger probing deeper beneath the lace.

"Don't." Landon grabbed my wrist, stopping my exploration. "Please don't say it if you don't mean it, Rufus. My heart can't take it."

"I do mean it," I promised, only just realising that I meant it. "I love you, Landon."

"Good," he said. "Because I lo–"

He never got to finish that sentence. Or maybe he did and I just didn't hear it. All I remember was the blaring of a horn. The driver swearing. The screech of metal on metal. Glass breaking.

And the world went black.

CHAPTER 22

I WAS DROWNING IN TREACLE. Fighting my way through thick, syrupy layers and trying to reach the surface. To reach consciousness. I tried to wake up. I really did. But every single part of my body felt leaden and unresponsive and it was all too much effort. Besides, I was warm and comfortable where I was, deep inside my own head. It was tempting to stay, lost in this cosy dream world where nothing and nobody could hurt me. What was the hurry to return to real life where nobody liked me anyway?

Landon likes you, a small voice told me. *Landon loves you.* That was what he'd been about to say before... Before what? Before I fell asleep? Was that what had happened? But it didn't sound like me. It didn't make sense. Why would anyone fall asleep in the middle of someone telling them they loved them? I remembered Landon though. Or did I? Images flashed through my mind in rapid succession. But they didn't seem to match up with me either. The man in my mind was fat and I'd never go for someone like that. I was too shallow. His eyes, though. Big, brown puppy dog eyes. I loved his eyes. I loved him. Didn't I? Why was it so damn hard to remember anything for longer than two seconds at a time?

Sometimes, there were voices, interrupting my dreams and trying to drag me back to the surface. Most sounded familiar, although I never seemed able to put a name or a face to any of them. Others, I didn't know at all. They talked to me. They talked about me. The words either made sense or they didn't.

Time was meaningless, floating in my mental abyss. There was no night or day. No light. Only ever the darkness. Inevitably though, the pull back to wakefulness became too strong to resist. The weight of my limbs eased. The treacle in my brain thinned. My eyes flickered open. And shut again because it was too much fucking effort.

"Killigan!" A woman's voice. It sounded familiar. Comforting. It sounded like home. I concentrated, but her name wouldn't come to me. "Did you see that? He opened his eyes."

"Are you sure?" That was a man. Killigan? That was what the woman called him. I frowned, because all I got when I tried to remember who Killigan might be, was a deep sense of dislike.

"There! You see that? He's frowning."

"Sweetheart, it's been three weeks. Maybe you're imagining things that you want to see, because you want so badly for him to wake up."

"I know what I saw, Killigan." I felt pressure on my arm. Warm and reassuring. A hand, maybe. "Rufus? Rufus, honey, it's Marcie. Can you open your eyes for me again?"

It wasn't easy, but I did it. I struggled to keep them open, because my heavy lids wanted to close. A woman leaned over me. There were tears in her eyes, but her face was kind. Concerned. A man hovered over her shoulder, heavy set and gruff looking. Marcie and Killigan. I remembered now. I lived with them. My lips moved, but no sound came out. Marcie squeezed my arm.

"Don't try and speak. There's a tube in your throat. Killigan, get the doctor."

Killigan looked like he wanted to say something, but then he turned and hurried out of the room. A hospital room, I could see that now. Why was I in hospital with a tube down my throat? And what did Killigan mean when he said it had been three weeks? He couldn't be talking about me, surely? I couldn't have been there for three weeks.

"Rufus, you're going to be okay," Marcie said. "Everyone is here for you. Well, in spirit if not in person. Your mum and dad are here. They went to the hotel to rest and change their clothes, but they'll come back as soon as we let them know you're awake. We've been taking it in turns to sit with you. Stefan is here. He's back at the house. Alex had to go home because of his job, but he came for the first few days after the accident. Eric and Mason stayed for as long as they could too, but they had to go back to America. Even Alison has visited when she can get away from the restaurant. It's not easy for her when she's so short-staffed, of course."

There were a lot of names in that little spiel that meant nothing to me. Mum and Dad were a given, but I drew a blank at the others. I had a feeling that Stefan ought to mean something to me, but right at that moment I couldn't even hazard a guess.

"Jesus, Marcie, don't talk the kid's ear off the second he opens his eyes." Killigan walked back into the room. There was a look of relief on his craggy features that I wasn't used to seeing, especially not when it was directed at me. "Doctor said she's on her way."

"Good. Now, go and phone Jerry and Claire."

"But I–" Marcie shot him a look over her shoulder that stopped Killigan in his tracks. He rolled his eyes and turned to leave again. "Fine, but just remember he's not yours, Marcie. You'll have to let other people get a look in at some point. Especially once his mother arrives."

"I know that," Marcie said, a tinge of pink creeping into her cheeks.

The more I looked at her, the more I remembered. Marcie was a mother hen, taking in waifs and strays who had nowhere else to go. Maybe that was who the others were. That list of names she spouted. Killigan was her boyfriend and he was a... what? A policeman. That was it.

A doctor arrived, bringing with her a number of nurses. They fussed around the bed, doing God only knows what, but by the time they had finished, at least the tube down my throat had gone. I was also exhausted, which gave me a genuine excuse not to answer any of the hundred and one questions the doctor fired at me. Maybe if I had been more with it, I would have confessed to the fact I couldn't answer because I couldn't remember shit from the accident or the events leading up to it. As it was, it was easier just to close my eyes and fall back asleep.

When I opened them again, there was a woman sat in a chair by my bed. A man stood over by the window. Marcie and Killigan had gone. I wished they hadn't left me alone because right then they were all that was familiar. They were like a security blanket to me. It took a few moments before the fuzziness in my head cleared and I recognised the new couple in my hospital room as my parents. Tears pricked my eyes as the realisation hit, because I was actually happy to see them. And I knew how much my mother hated coming to London, so that was another memory right there. It was good to know that things were coming back to me slowly.

Mum cried when I woke up and Dad came to stand at the end of the bed, looking emotional as he stared down at me. Mum talked almost as much as Marcie, although her chatter was all about her and Dad and what they'd been up to since I'd seen them last. There was little I heard that was of any interest, but at least she didn't just sit there spouting a whole bunch of names of people I couldn't remember.

I was saved when the door opened and a blond whirling-dervish launched itself across the room and literally right onto my bed. Automatically, my arms came up and around the slight figure and held him close. He lifted his head and I found myself looking into bright green eyes. This was Stefan, I knew that without a doubt. It was as though the man was ingrained on my heart and soul. I hadn't recognised his name when Marcie first said, but I'd know him anywhere once I saw him in person. And that had to be a good sign, didn't it? That I remembered people when I saw them?

"Oh, sweetheart, I really don't think you should be on the bed," my mother said worriedly.

"Sorry, this is what he does," Killigan said from the doorway. Although he sounded amused rather than concerned. "I think he has a thing for patients in hospital beds."

"Excuse me!" Stefan said indignantly, sitting up cross-legged on the side of my bed. "The only time I've done it before was when Alex was stabbed. And this is Rufus. You make it sound like I go around hospitals accosting random strangers."

"Yeah, whatever. Get off the bed, Stefan," Killigan said with a snort.

"But I have to check my Rufie is okay," Stefan whined, sticking out his bottom lip in a perfect pout.

"He'd be better without you sitting on him," Killigan remarked dryly. "Come on, Stefan. Do you really want me to tell Alex that you're not behaving yourself? After you promised..."

"Fine." Stefan scooted hastily off of the bed on the opposite side to where my mother sat. Grabbing my hand, he leaned over and kissed me on the cheek. "He's such a big meanie," he stage-whispered, fully intending for everyone else to hear.

Now that I'd seen Stefan, I remembered the man he'd recently married too. The fearsome Alex Gill. I'd never understood the hold the brute had over my best friend, but Stefan loved him. Adored him even. Alex told him what to do and Stefan did it. It worked for them. They were in love and so happy it made cynics like me nauseous. At the same time, I envied their relationship. That kind of love was what I wanted for myself. I wanted someone to look at me and see the centre of their world. I thought I'd found it with... with who? The name escaped me momentarily, but even so, I couldn't shake the feeling that I'd been on the cusp of something good right before I'd ended up in a hospital bed.

"L-landon..." I murmured, my voice hoarse. That was the name at the forefront of my fragile mind. Yet still the only image I could muster up was of some fat guy. *A fat guy in purple lace knickers.* Well, shit. Where had that come from? And why the hell did I find the thought sexy rather than it making me want to puke my guts up? I had to know who Landon was and what he meant to me. "W-where...?"

"Rufus, I'm not sure you're ready..." Killigan began before my mother interrupted.

"To think we liked that boy when you brought him home," she scoffed. "He walked away from the accident with nothing more than a few cuts and bruises. Hasn't even had the decency to call and see how you are. And I really thought he cared about you."

I switched my gaze to Stefan's and raised my eyebrows in question. He shrugged.

"We all thought he cared, Rufus," he said quietly. "But it's true. He went back to his parents and nobody has heard from him since."

"Oh."

I didn't know why it hurt so much. Why there was a sudden crushing pain in my chest that refused to budge. I could barely remember the man, so why should I care so much that he'd waked away from me and not looked back? Tears leaked from my eyes, but I couldn't speak. My throat felt like it was closing up. I started to sweat profusely and I looked at Stefan, panic building as I silently pleaded with him to help me. Everything hurt. I wanted to puke, but I didn't dare because I knew if I did, I'd choke. My fingers closed in a vice-like grip around Stefan's wrist.

"Rufus? Rufus, what is it? What's wrong?"

I didn't know who said that. Maybe it was all of them at once. Maybe it was none of them and the questions were in my own head. So dizzy. Couldn't think. Couldn't breathe. Stefan faded from view and my last thought was that I was really in trouble here.

CHAPTER 23

It took gargantuan effort, but I was finally able to peel my eyes open. A nurse leaned over me, her face smiling and kind. My chest still hurt and I was tired. So, so tired. I wanted to go back to sleep, but the nurse seemed quite pleased that I was awake, so I tried to keep my eyes open. Look at me, doing something to make someone else happy. Go, Rufus!

"Rufus, do you know where you are?"

I nodded weakly. Hospital, although it was a different room to before and a whole new set of machines beeped steadily at the bedside.

"What...? Wh...where...?" I tried, but my tongue felt leaden and too big for my mouth. The words were jumbled in my fuzzy brain and wouldn't come.

"Honey, you had a heart attack," the nurse said gently. "You're on the coronary care unit, so we can monitor you for a couple of days." She smiled again. "There's quite a few people waiting in the family room who will be happy to have you back with us. Happy and relieved. You gave them all quite a scare."

Me too, I thought, but didn't say it out loud. Talking required more energy than I currently possessed.

"The doctors still have some tests to run," the nurse continued. "But I can send someone in to see you in the meantime. Only one at a time though. We don't want anybody exhausting you, do we?"

Too late for that. I was already done in. A fucking heart attack and I wasn't even thirty. My life was over. I felt the hot sting of tears of self-pity and couldn't be bothered to even try and brush them away.

"Oh, sweetheart. You're young and healthy," the nurse said sympathetically, using a tissue to wipe the tears from my cheek. "The doctors expect you to make a full recovery, so you have to look to the future with optimism, okay? Now, who would you like me to send in? The blond boy is very pretty, but perhaps a little excitable. How about we start with your mum?"

I shook my head and turned my face to the pillow. I didn't want to see anybody, to have them feeling sorry for me. For the rest of the day, I refused to have any visitors. In the end they stopped asking. I think the nurse told them all to go home as the stress wasn't good for my heart. When I woke from a late evening nap, Killigan was sat in the chair beside my bed. I wasn't even surprised. He'd never been the sort of man to take no for an answer.

"Shouldn't you be out catching criminals," I croaked.

Killigan gave a rare smile, before reaching over to the bedside cabinet and pouring some water into a plastic cup. He held the cup to my lips and I drank gratefully, the cool liquid soothing my parched throat. Setting the cup back down on the cabinet, Killigan leaned forward in his chair and took hold of my hand.

"I took some leave," he said. "I told them my adopted son had been in an accident. And before you say anything, I know you've got a dad and I know he's here for you, but... well, I'm here too. I just want you to know that, Rufus. God, when I thought we'd lost you..."

"I'm still here."

"And you have no idea how glad I am to hear it. Promise me you won't be going for third-time-lucky."

I snorted. "I never went for the first two times. In fact, I don't even know what happened to begin with."

"You don't remember?" Killigan raised his eyebrows.

"More than I did, but not all of it."

"Tell me the bits you do remember," he said, sounding very much like the police officer he really was.

"Uh... there was the concert," I began hesitantly, hoping I was right about that much and it hadn't all been some crazy coma-induced dream. I felt that my memory was returning more and more, but at the same time I worried bits of it were a trick of the mind. "I was with... Landon." I remembered him now. It still seemed unlikely that I would be interested in someone like him, but deep down I knew it was true. I liked him more than I'd ever liked anyone. "He wore them, you know."

Killigan looked confused. "Wore what?"

"The knickers. He wore them for our date."

"He did? No wonder his parents kicked off the way they did when they arrived at the hospital that night."

"Eric set me up," I told Killigan, frowning as that particular detail came back to me. Beside my bed, the heart monitor suddenly started to beep faster. Killigan's eyes widened with concern, so I forced myself to calm down before he called in a nurse and had me sedated or something. I was still angry though, about what Eric had done. "He got one of the band members to come on to me. He wanted to see how fast I would drop Landon when I got a better offer."

"That little shitbag. Somehow, he forgot to mention that little fact when he came to the hospital," Killigan said, sounding annoyed. "So, what did you do?"

"I left." I didn't blame him if he was suspicious. Not given my track record. "For me, Landon *is* the better offer. At least... I thought he was."

"Yes, well, we'll talk about Landon in a minute. How much do you remember about the accident?"

I screwed up my face in concentration, but nothing came to mind other than a flash of purple lace and an aborted 'I love you'. Well, good. I was glad he never got to say it, because it would obviously have been a lie. If he'd meant it, he would have called to see how I was, even if he couldn't get to the hospital to see for himself that I was still breathing.

"Nothing really. I think we got a taxi." I looked at Killigan uncertainly. "Did we?"

"You did," Killigan confirmed. "Only, it wasn't licensed and the driver was pissed as a fart. He ran a red light and a delivery truck smashed into your side of the car. That's why you were hurt more than Landon and the driver."

I nodded my understanding. The doctors had already explained to me that I'd suffered a major head trauma, one that had left me in a three-week long coma and would probably result in the left side of my body being permanently weaker than the right. It was possible I would regain some of strength in time, but it was too early to tell when or how much. The heart attack hadn't helped, of course. There was a long road to recovery ahead of me. It was no wonder Landon had walked away from me and not looked back. Who, in their right mind, would want a broken mess like me?

"So... about Landon..." Killigan began.

"I don't blame him," I said quickly, even as my eyes became wet with the sting of tears. "I wasn't easy to live with before. Now look at me. I'm broken. Head. Heart." Subconsciously, I used my right hand to rub my near useless left arm. "No man is going to want me now."

"You'll get over this, Rufus." Killigan patted my shoulder. "But Landon... I don't think he left you. Not willingly, at least."

"Then where is he?"

"After the accident, his parents came to the hospital. They didn't seem to care Landon had just survived a serious crash. They were furious. With Landon and with you. *Especially* with you. Sod the fact you were still in resuscitation. The doctors were still fighting to keep you alive and those bastards stood there blaming you for what happened. Anyway, once Landon was patched up, they insisted he left with them. Told him Marcie and I wouldn't have time to take care of him what with you being in here. He argued, because he didn't want to go, but they kept piling on the emotional pressure. Perhaps I should have stood up for him, I don't know, but my mind was you at the time. In the end, I didn't even see them leave."

"I don't get it." My head hurt too much to think. I knew there were stitches down the left side of my scalp, but I hadn't put a hand up there to feel yet. They'd shaved half of my head too and I dreaded being faced with a mirror. I might not have long, silken locks like Stefan, but I still felt the loss of my hair. I was probably as ugly as fucking sin without it. "What are you saying?"

"I'm saying..." Killigan said slowly, "... that I think Landon's parents have stopped him coming back to the hospital. I've tried calling him, but his phone is off. I even drove over there and knocked on the door. His snooty mother answered and said he didn't want to see me or have anything else to do with you."

"Well then..."

"I don't believe her, Rufus," Killigan said firmly. "And I won't believe it until I hear it from Landon himself. Which isn't going to happen, because I can't get anywhere near him."

"You mean like... what? They're keeping him a prisoner?"

"Maybe. I don't know for sure. But it would explain why he hasn't even called to ask how you are?"

I shook my head and closed my eyes. I wanted to believe there was a reason why Landon hadn't called or visited me in the hospital, but it didn't matter anyway. He was better off without me. I was damaged and weak and ugly and it would have been best for everyone if I'd just died. From the head injury. From the heart attack. Who the fuck cared? I had nothing to live for anyway.

CHAPTER 24

ANOTHER TEN DAYS passed before they would discharge me from the hospital. The head was healing nicely and Stefan had tidied up my hair on one of his visits. Alex had come in to see me at the weekend before taking Stefan home with him. After all the years of animosity between us, I thought we might start to actually like each other if we weren't careful. Alison had visited one evening and reassured me that my job at the restaurant would be there waiting whenever I was ready to return to work. Most days, my parents and Killigan and Marcie took it in turns to sit with me. Mum and Dad tried hard to persuade me to return home with them while I recuperated and were hurt when I told them I wanted to stay in London. I regretted upsetting them, but they grudgingly accepted my decision when I claimed that I wasn't up to what could be a two to three hours long journey by the time we got out of the city.

There was still no word from Landon. Killigan had been to the house again, with no more success than the previous time. He'd even sat in his car at the end of the driveway for a couple of hours, but Landon had not appeared. I hadn't told any of them, but as soon as I was able, I intended going to Landon's house myself and climbing through a window if they wouldn't let me in the door.

Being home felt strange at first. I'd expected to feel a sense of relief at being home in my own bed again, but I didn't. Pleased as I was to leave the hospital, it had been a month since I'd set foot in the house. It felt like when I first moved in. All my clothes and belongings were there, but I was a stranger in someone else's home. My parents stayed two more days then went home, promising to return soon. Once they'd gone, I went upstairs to lie on my bed and breathed a guilty sigh of relief that I was finally alone for the first time since waking from my coma.

I slept through the night and went down the next morning to find Killigan had already left for work. Marcie was in the kitchen, preparing breakfast. I stared at her offering in horror when she put a bowl of muesli on the table in front of me.

"What the fuck?" I grumbled.

"Language," she said. "And it's good for you. No more fry ups or fatty foods for you. Coffee is out as well. No caffeine. We have to protect that heart of yours, don't we?"

"By feeding me cardboard?" I pushed the offending muesli around the bowl unenthusiastically.

"Rufus, honey..." Marcie sighed and pulled up the chair next to mine. She reached over and rubbed my arm. "You have to get yourself well. And if that means exercise and healthy eating then that's what you're going to do."

"What's the point?" I asked bitterly, annoyed that I was close to crying again. It was all I ever seemed to do these days.

"The point is," Marcie said, "you are precious, Rufus,

and to a lot of people. We want you around for a long to come, so you need to look after yourself."

"You might care," I retorted sullenly, shoving the bowl across the table. "Not so sure I do. My life is over. I'll never become a chef with a gammy left arm, will I? And sex is out, right? Nobody's going to take a chance on fucking the guy who had a heart attack."

"Oh, sweetheart." Marcie wrapped her arms around me and I rested my head on her shoulder, because it felt nice to be held. Annoyingly, the tears started again, but I let them fall rather than brushing them away. "I've been reading up about all of this online and it's perfectly natural to feel depressed after a heart attack, especially at your age. You're scared it could happen again and that's understandable."

"For fuck's sake, I'm not depressed." I pulled away from her and got up from the table. I'd rather go hungry than have to eat that slop. "I'm angry."

"Rufus..." Marcie stretched a hand towards me and I jerked backwards, beyond her reach.

"I'm angry with Eric for setting me up. I'm angry with the taxi driver for running that stupid red light and ruining my life. I'm angry with myself for getting in that bloody car in the first place and..." I ground the heels of my hands into my wet eyes, trying to stem the flow of frustrated tears. "I'm angry that I don't do anything but cry these days and – most of all – I'm angry with Landon. So angry I can't fucking breathe." I dropped to my knees in the middle of the kitchen floor and sobbed. "Why did he leave me, Marcie? How could he do that?"

"I don't know, love."

Marcie knelt on the floor in front of me and this time when she reached for me, I let her pull me back into her embrace. We stayed like that for the longest time, clinging to each other while we both cried. In some small way, it was comforting to know that, seeing my heart was breaking, Marcie's heart broke for me at the same time. Finally, I had no tears left to cry. My back was aching and my knees hurt from the hard floor. I was sure Marcie had to be as uncomfortable as I was, so reluctantly, I peeled my puffy, reddened face from the shoulder of her now soggy sweater and sat back on my heels.

"Sorry," I mumbled, wiping my snotty nose on my sleeve.

"You've nothing to be sorry for," Marcie said firmly. "Now, I don't know why that boy walked away from you, but we're going to find out."

"How?" I looked at her in miserable confusion.

"Well, first, you are going to eat something. Don't worry, I'll find something better than muesli." She smiled, helping me to my feet. "Bloody awful stuff. Can't imagine what I was thinking in the first place. Then I want you to get cleaned up. Make yourself look beautiful. Put on some make-up and some purple and then you and I are going to pay Mr. Holby a visit."

I ate the second breakfast Marcie served without argument, although I barely tasted it. Then I hurried upstairs to change, before Marcie could change her mind to about taking me to Landon's house. My little melt-down in the kitchen had left me exhausted and the whole left-hand side of my body felt extra weak and shaky. If Marcie noticed she'd probably send me back to bed and I wouldn't be going anywhere.

I fought my way into a white t-shirt and tugged a deep purple button-down shirt over the top, only to find my left hand refused to cooperate and do up the buttons. Tearing off the shirt, I threw it across the room with a growl of frustration, but at least I didn't cry. Then again, I wasn't sure I had any more tears in me.

As if by magic, Marcie appeared in the bedroom doorway. Casually, she bent down to pick the shirt up from the floor.

"What a beautiful colour. Is this what you're going to wear?"

"It was," I muttered. "Except I can't do the buttons up."

Marcie held out the shirt.

"Would you allow me to do them up for you?" Grudgingly, I nodded and let her help me slip the shirt back on. "You do know there's no shame in asking for help when you need it, don't you?"

"I know," I said quietly, shamefaced as Marcie began to fasten the buttons. "I just don't want to feel like I'm being a nuisance."

"And now he grows a conscience," Marcie replied, laughing. "Listen, it's not forever. You'll be back to your usual self in no time. But, until then, let me mother you a bit, okay? Now, where is that nice sparkly eyeshadow of yours? It will go perfectly with that shirt."

I drew the line at her putting my make-up on for me. I was right-handed anyway, so that was one task that I could manage by myself. She did brush my hair though and I was fine with that, even if I wasn't so happy with the fact the close cropped hairstyle I now sported was my natural mousy brown. Although, once I was finished with my make-up, I thought having short hair made my eyes look bigger and my lips seem poutier, so maybe it wasn't a total disaster after all.

Marcie insisted I wore a coat. I insisted I didn't want one. We compromised with a lightweight denim jacket that was a few shades lighter than my dark purple shirt. Finally, once I had donned my purple Doc Martens, with Marcie tying the laces, and Marcie had put on her own shoes and grabbed her bag, we were ready to leave.

Eagerly rushing out of the front door, I ran smack into Killigan's barrelled chest. Luckily, he caught me before I could bounce off him and hit the deck. He held onto my arms, scowling between me and Marcie.

"And where the bloody hell do you think you're going?" he asked.

CHAPTER 25

IN THE END, Killigan drove, but only after a doorstep scene worthy of a soap opera, I told him where we were going. He said over his dead body. I pointed out it was more likely to be over my dead body seeing as I was the one with the bad heart. That made Marcie cry which made Killigan angry. I cried too, but admittedly, it was the fake crying I did to get my own way. Like I said – all cried out. Anyway, Marcie and Killigan fell for it and because they were worried about me, what with the dodgy ticker and all, they didn't want me to get stressed. So, despite the fact he thought it could only stress me out even more, Killigan agreed to take me to see Landon.

As we turned into the end of Landon's long driveway my heart sank into my purple boots. There was a 'sold' sign next to the gate and two removal vans parked outside the house. A mountain of boxes and furniture was strewn across the lawn, waiting to be loaded. I couldn't see Landon anywhere, but Mrs. Holby stood on the steps, instructing the removals men on how to do their job. There was a younger woman with her, who I assumed to be Landon's sister.

"Fuck," Killigan said under his breath.

For once, Marcie didn't reprimand him for swearing, probably because she was thinking the same thing. 'Fuck' just about summed up this shitfest of a situation.

"Rufus, wait a damn minute, will you?" Killigan called out as I opened the car door.

I ignored him and climbed out anyway, bemused by the look of shock on the faces of Landon's mother and sister as I walked towards them. I don't know why they were so surprised to see me. They must have known I'd show up at some point once I got out of the hospital, although it was obvious they had planned to move out before that could happen. The sister's face was a picture and I'd never even met her.

"Mother, you said–"

"Be quiet, Sarah," Mrs. Holby snapped. "Go inside and make sure your brother stays in his room."

"I want to see him," I said.

From the corner of my eye, I could see the removal men had stopped work to watch whatever spectacle that was about to unfold. Given the way Mrs. Holby had been talking to them when we arrived, they were probably hoping to see her get her comeuppance.

"Absolutely not!" Mrs. Holby spat, as her daughter turned obediently and walked into the house. "Please leave immediately or I shall be forced to call the police."

"I am the police, love," Killigan said, coming up behind me. "As I've told you every other time I've been here. Now, I would really like to speak to Landon regarding the accident."

"Then get a warrant," Mrs Holby retorted in a frosty tone. "Just as I have told *you* on previous occasions, Detective."

"I don't need a warrant. Your son is a victim, not a suspect."

Mrs. Holby pursed her lips and glared at Killigan like he'd just taken a dump on her doorstep or something.

"Well, as you can see, it really isn't convenient at this precise moment. If it is genuinely necessary for Landon to speak to the police again, perhaps I could arrange a time to bring him to the station."

"But I'm here now," Killigan argued. "And I will only take a few minutes of Landon's time."

"I'm sorry, Detective, but I cannot and will not allow you to speak to my son." Mrs. Holby's glacial gaze flicked in my direction. "Especially not while *that* is present."

"Oh, you don't need to worry about him." Killigan put his hands on my shoulders and squeezed, his way of telling me to keep my big mouth shut. "He's still got amnesia from the accident. Doesn't remember a thing."

"But he asked to see Landon," Mrs. Holby said, unconvinced.

Killigan pinched me. I gave her a blank stare and said, "Who's Landon?"

"But..."

"Brain damage," Killigan put in quickly. "Most likely permanent. The boy's got the attention span of a goldfish."

"Even so, I would prefer that he's not present should I decide to let you see my son."

"Okay, if that's the way it has to be. Rufus, go and wait in the car."

I wanted to argue, but I had to trust Killigan and believe

he had some sort of game plan. Quite frankly, I'd stand on my head and whistle Dixie if it meant I got to see Landon, even from a distance.

"Rufus?"

The hesitant voice came from the open front door. All three of us jerked around to see Landon standing there, staring at me in uncertainty. His sister was at his side, holding onto his arm, more as a gesture of support than restraint. She'd gone against their mother's wishes, told him I was outside and brought him to me. Landon had lost a lot of weight since I'd last seen him, but it didn't look good on him. He looked positively ill with dark shadows beneath haunted brown eyes.

"Landon, go back inside at once," Mrs. Holby ordered sharply, stepping in front of him as if to block his view.

Landon and his sister simply stepped around her and walked down the steps. Landon's eyes never left mine, but he made no move to touch me.

"You're here," he said. "How can you be here?"

"Killigan brought me," I answered, although I got the impression my mode of transport wasn't really what he was asking about.

It wasn't turning out to be the reunion I'd hoped for. Landon didn't seem happy to see me, nor did he seem annoyed that I'd tracked him down. Overall, he appeared to be totally stunned that I was there at all.

"I don't understand." Landon reached out a hand and then dropped to his side again without making contact. His gaze raked over me from head to foot. "What's wrong with your arm?"

"Oh, this?" I glanced down to where I held my left arm cradled against my chest, as I had become prone to doing over the past few days. It was not only comfortable, but it made it less obvious to onlookers that the arm was pretty much non-functional. "After effect of the accident. The doctors say it will improve with time."

I had to throw that into the mix, thinking maybe if he knew my disability was only temporary, he might be more inclined to take me back.

"Landon, I insist," his mother said, her voice rising to an ear-splitting screech. "Go back to the house immediately. I won't tell you again."

"Oh, Mother... if you don't like it, *you* go back inside," Sarah retorted. "After what you did, you should be hiding yourself away in shame anyway."

"What did she do?" Killigan asked keenly, the detective in him jumping on the remark in an instant. Landon and I were still too busy staring at each other to pass comment.

"It was nothing," Mrs. Holby said quickly. "It was for Landon's own good..."

"She told us Rufus was dead." Sarah glared at her mother, before turning to me with a sympathetic look on her face. "Landon has spent the last month believing you died in that accident. She even said he couldn't go to the funeral because your family didn't want him there."

"Sarah, stop!" Mrs Holby was red in the face with rage. "And, Landon, go to your room. I will not be disobeyed like this. Just wait until I tell your father..."

"Woman, there's something wrong with you," Killigan ground out furiously. "Landon's a grown man, for God's sake. And I'll tell you now, you can move house and lock him in his room as often and for as long as you like, but your son will still be gay."

Mrs. Holby was not to be deterred. Clearly, she saw

nothing wrong in her actions and her refusal to accept Landon's sexuality was resolute.

"I'm phoning my husband," she said haughtily. "And I'll have you disbarred, Detective, or whatever it is they do to corrupt police officers."

"That's it, Mother. We're going back into the house." Sarah let go off Landon's arm and took hold of her mother's instead. As she led Mrs. Holby away, she turned to look over her shoulder at Killigan. "Please take care of my brother, Detective." Her gaze landed on me and she smiled. "I hope you can forgive him. None of this was his fault."

"There's nothing to forgive."

She nodded, before forcible dragging her mother up the steps and into the house, followed by a round of applause from the watching removals men.

"Landon, do you want to come with us?"

Killigan stepped forward and lightly placed his hand on Landon's arm. Jealousy sparked, a sharp pain in the centre of my chest, that Killigan should be the first one to touch him. To make the contact that I longed to make, but I didn't seem able to move towards him any more than Landon did with me. All we could do was stand and stare at each other in awe, like neither one of us could believe the other was standing there.

Landon nodded in answer to Killigan's question.

"Come on then, let's get you home."

Killigan steered Landon towards the car and I followed. Marcie jumped out at our approach, running over to Landon and hugging him tightly.

"I think he's in shock." Killigan told her. "I'll tell you everything when we get home, once the boys are settled with mugs of your special hot chocolate. They're both in dire need, I would say."

In the car, Landon continued to stare at me, like I was something new and wonderful he'd never seen before. After a few minutes, my brain finally clicked into gear and I reached across the seat to clasp his hand in mine. His gaze dropped to where our fingers were linked and stayed there for the entire journey home.

CHAPTER 26

LANDON and I sat side by side on the sofa, our bodies joined at arm, hip and thigh. In our hands, we cradled mugs of steaming hot chocolate. I had heard Alex say once that Marcie's special blend of hot chocolate was magical and could cure any wrong, be it of the heart or head. It had sound overly sentimental, especially coming from that big oaf, but I had to concede, he had a point. That day, we both had whipped cream and sprinkles on top, so I assumed Killigan had told her during their whispered conversation in the kitchen, exactly what Landon's sister and bitch of a mother had said.

Still, we had not really spoken, but since that initial contact in the car, it was as though we couldn't bear to be without some degree of physical connection. I simply had to be touching him, and as he had yet to pull away, I guess he felt the same way.

Killigan and Marcie came into the room, probably concerned by the lack of conversation going on. Marcie joined us on the sofa, sitting beside me and putting her hand on my leg. Killigan perched on the armchair opposite, leaning forward as if to demonstrate the seriousness of what he was about to say. Instinctively, I pressed closer to Landon's side, certain whatever it was would be more bad news.

"Marcie and I want you both to know," Killigan began earnestly, "that you have a home here for as long as you want it, whether you're together as partners or not. Although, given the way you're sitting, I'm guessing you at least want to make a go of things."

"We do," I said, speaking for the both of us.

Beside me, Landon nodded in agreement and a faint smile of approval ghosted across Killigan's lips. Marcie squeezed my leg in silent encouragement.

"Good," Killigan continued. "What happened to the two of you was horrific, but I hope you can get through it together. Landon, you're the best thing to ever happen to Rufus and I believe he's been good for you too. And I'm so sorry your mother lied to you. I promise you, if I had any idea, I would have found a way of getting you out of that house long before today."

"She said he was dead," Landon murmured quietly. He sounded so matter-of-fact. Not upset or angry. Most likely, Killigan was right about him being in shock. He was probably still trying to get his head around the fact I was cuddled up to him on the sofa after he'd spent the last month in mourning for me. "She said the accident was my fault and that's why you didn't want anything to do with me."

"Oh, sweetheart, that was never true," Marcie said, shedding the tears that Landon didn't seem able to at that moment in time. "I tried calling, but your phone was switched off."

"Mother took my phone away," Landon admitted, shame-faced.

"And Killigan went to your house so many times and was constantly turned away."

Landon blinked at her in surprise. "I never knew that. Mother never once said that he'd been there."

"I told you," Marcie said accusingly, turning to Killigan. "We should have sent Alex round there."

"If she wouldn't let the police in, she wouldn't have let Alex in either, would she?" Killigan countered, rolling his eyes.

"Don't be so sure of that," Marcie snorted. "People don't tend to say no to Alex if they know what's good for them."

"I do," I said.

"Yeah, right before you run and hide behind me for protection," Killigan scoffed.

Landon surprised us all by giggling.

"God, I missed this."

"Well, get used to it," Killigan grinned. "Because this is your home now."

"After you get back from my brother's, of course."

"What?" Now, all three of us rounded on Marcie with confused looks. "But you said he could stay. Why are you sending him away again?"

"I'm sending you both away. You need some time together to mend. My brother has a guest house that will be just perfect for you."

"You mean that skanky room over Tony's garage?" I raised my eyebrows sceptically.

"No, of course not. I mean my other brother, Roger. He lives just outside of Cardiff with his partner, Troy."

"Wait, so how come you never mentioned him before?" I asked, because being a self-appointed surrogate mother to a growing number of young, gay men, you'd expect her to have mentioned at some point, the fact she had a brother who also happened to be that way inclined.

"Oh, I'm sure I've talked about him plenty of times," Marcie replied airily. "Anyway, it's only for a couple of weeks. Then you can come home."

"And get back to work," Killigan added in a smug tone. "Landon, I don't know how much, if any, of your stuff we can get back from your parents. I can lend you the money to buy some clothes if necessary. I'm sure Alison will give you your old job back at the restaurant, if you want it."

"What about me?" I asked, because I wasn't sure I was up to returning to work just yet, not while my left arm was still next to useless.

"While you're recovering physically, you don't have to go out to work," Killigan answered. "But I expect you to help out around the house as much as you're able. A few of your meals wouldn't go amiss either."

"Okay," I agreed happily, relieved that he wasn't going to pressure me into something I didn't feel I was ready for. Doing stuff around the house wouldn't be as stressful as being in the restaurant kitchen. "So, when do we leave for Cardiff?"

"I'll drive you down on Saturday," Marcie said. "Killigan has to work, but I could do with a weekend away after the last month or so."

"That will give us a chance to get Landon some clobber," Killigan added. "In smaller sizes, by the look of it."

"Yeah, don't lose any more weight," I scolded Landon gently. "I might not love you if you get too skinny."

"Darling, he needs to be healthy." Marcie patted my thigh before giving Landon a reassuring smile.

"He can be fat and healthy, like Killigan."

"Rufus..."

"It's fine," Landon spoke up. "I promise I won't lose any more weight if you promise to dye your hair purple again."

"Done."

I smiled, certain that was a promise I would keep so long as the dye wasn't harmful to the fresh scar on my scalp. Silently, I made another promise to myself to research some recipes that would feed my man up a bit whilst keeping his heart healthy at the same time.

We finished our drinks and dutifully carried the mugs out to the kitchen to wash and put away in the cupboard and prove to Killigan we were doing our bit. As Landon was about to go back to Marcie and Killigan in the living room, I grabbed his hand and dragged him towards the stairs instead. Once inside my bedroom, with the door securely closed behind us, I pushed him onto the bed and straddled his legs. Despite his obvious weight loss, I was pleased to find he still carried a lot of meat on his chunky thighs and it was a stretch to seat myself on him comfortably.

"Rufus, we can't," he persisted weakly, as I tugged on the waistband of the tatty old jogging bottoms he wore.

"I'm fine," I said impatiently, because having only one functional hand was seriously impeding my progress. "The doctor said light exercise is good for me. I'm not going to have another heart attack."

"I was talking about Killigan being right downstairs." Landon grabbed my wrists between both hands. "And what the fuck do you mean by *another* heart attack?"

Shit. I'd forgotten he believed me to have died in the accident. There was no way he could have known about the heart attack when it had happened after I came out of the coma he hadn't even known I was in. He thought I was already six feet under by that point.

"It was only a little one," I told him nonchalantly. It wasn't a total lie. The fact I was still around, walking and talking, proved it couldn't have been that major, surely? "So long as I don't get too excited, there shouldn't be a problem."

"Shouldn't be?" Landon echoed. Letting go off my wrists, he lifted me off him and dumped me on the bed. "That's it, I'm definitely not having sex with you now. How do you propose we do it without you getting excited?"

"A *bit* of excitement is okay," I argued. "Besides, I never said anything about full on sex. I was just going to blow you as a welcome home present."

"Some present if it kills you in the process. No way. I'm not doing it, Rufus. I only just got you back."

"And I only just got you back. That's why I need to do this. I need to make you mine again."

I could see the indecision in his brown eyes. He wanted it as much as I did, but he was afraid something would go wrong and he would lose me again. I was apprehensive too – I'd be stupid not to be – but I honestly felt fine. The need to re-establish our connection on an intimate level far outweighed any health concerns I might have.

I slipped my hand into Landon's joggers and this time he didn't resist. Encouraged, I knelt up on the bed and worked his waistband down far enough to free his dick. For all his protestations, he was already half-hard, his length thickened under my gaze alone and I lowered my head to suck the tip between my lips. A moment later, Landon gasped as I took him all the way into my mouth, sealing my lips around his thick girth.

His pubes tickled my nose and, briefly, it crossed my mind that a bit of manscaping was in order. But then Landon thrust his hips slightly and all else was forgotten other than giving my man the pleasure he deserved.

CHAPTER 27

ROGER WAS nothing like I expected. He was the oldest of the three siblings and differed greatly from both Marcie and Tony in appearance. He was only slightly taller than me, but a lot rounder, with wisps of white hair forming a halo around his bald palette. Pale blue eyes peered at us through silver-rimmed spectacles and I thought he looked older than the fifty-five years Marcie informed us he was. He was friendly though, and welcoming, quick to assure us that our being there would not be a bother.

His partner, Troy, was the same age, but looked younger. He struck me as quite trendy with his short dark hair gelled into spikes and his slim figure. His facial features were fairly rugged other than for his bright blue eyes that sparkled with mischief.

They seemed to be a mismatched pair, but from the way they looked at each other, it was clear they were very much in love.

"Twenty-one years," Troy said proudly, when Landon asked how long they had been together. "Roger worked at a local quarry and I was a truck driver. Our eyes met over ten tonnes of gritting sand and the rest is history."

"Didn't your families mind?" Landon asked quietly.

There was a sadness in his tone and I knew, however much he hated his family for the things they had done, he still loved and missed them too.

"Roger's family didn't bat an eyelid," Troy told him. "I wasn't so lucky. My parents disowned me on the spot and I never saw them or my sister again. Don't even know if they're still alive. I understand you're at the start of that same journey now, Landon, and I can't promise the hurt will ever go away completely. You learn to live with it though, and you build a new family with the people who love and accept you for who you are."

Tears filled Landon's eyes, but I knew he appreciated Troy's words. I understood now, why Marcie had brought us here to these two men rather than to Tony. Tony was a good man who didn't care in the slightest about a person's sexuality, but he hadn't lived through what we were going through. He could and would support us, but he'd never fully understand how it felt to be hated because of who we were.

Added to that, there was the similarity between Roger and Troy's relationship and mine and Landon's. I think Marcie wanted me to see that you didn't have to both be beautiful people for a relationship to work out. Landon was beautiful to me though, so that was a lesson that didn't need to be learned.

The guest house was not what I'd envisaged either. I'd expected a small outbuilding in the grounds of their home, but no. It was an actual guest house, as in a three-storey B&B. Roger and Troy had their private quarters on the ground floor and the upstairs rooms were all en-suite guest rooms. Marcie had a room on the second floor, alongside a couple who had come from up North somewhere. Mine and Landon's room was on the top floor, with a panoramic view of the sea and the Jurassic coastline.

Troy carried my bag upstairs for me and put the it on the large double bed.

"It gets better, you know," he said, nodding to where my left arm was cradled against my chest. I was puffing slightly too, out of breath from climbing two flights of stairs. "I had a heart attack five years ago. It took time, but I got back to full strength in the end. I'm sure you will too."

"I hope so," I said, deciding not to mention the fact the weakness stemmed as much from the brain damage sustained in the accident than the subsequent heart attack.

"I like your hair too," Roger said coming into the room behind us. "Remember when my hair was like that, Troy?"

"Babe, your hair was *never* like that," Troy teased. "You were already bald by the time you were twenty-five."

"Hey, I'm not bald!" Roger objected, running his fingers through the thin white strands and tossing his head back as though he still had long, curly locks. "And don't believe him anyway, boys. I was twenty-six."

The first evening we were there, Marcie drove us into Cardiff. The three of us had a meal and a stroll around the Bay area. It took a while to register, but eventually I realized I was paying no attention to whether people were looking at us or not. That was because I didn't care anymore. Let them stare if they had nothing better to do with their lives. Life was too short to concern myself with the judgement of others. Being with Landon was everything to me now, and more important than the opinion of strangers. Landon seemed more at ease in his own body too. I hoped it was because he felt the same way.

On Sunday, Roger and Troy invited us to have lunch with them. Shortly after, Marcie left for London, with Roger's parting suggestion that she propose to Killigan no doubt still ringing in her ears. I was all for it, but Landon thought she should stick to tradition and wait for Killigan to do the asking. I wondered what that meant for us. Who would be asking and who would be waiting. Then I shut that train of thought down fast, because it was way too soon to be thinking of weddings and shit.

Roger and Troy were preparing for new guests who were due to arrive that afternoon, so once we had waved our goodbyes to Marcie, Landon and I headed for the beach. There was not a grain of sand in sight, just dark grey rocks of varying sizes as far as the eye could see. I quite appreciated the rugged beauty of it all, whereas Landon complained the rocks were hard to walk on and he'd rather go to Barry Island where the beach was sandy.

Again, our perspectives differed and I went from thinking about marriage to wondering if our relationship could survive if we didn't seem to agree on anything. I guess the real test would come when we decided we wanted different things out of life. But, for now at least, all we wanted was each other, so we'd probably be okay for a while yet.

As we walked, Landon held my hand, helping me over some of the trickier rock formations we came across on our course. We walked the entire length of the beach, finally climbing a grassy embankment and finding ourselves at the side of a large playing field. People walked their dogs around the edges and there were several spectators watching a lively game of rugby on the field.

Landon noticed that my breathing had changed even before I did. He dragged me over to a wooden bench and ordered me to sit and rest before we attempted the long walk back to the guesthouse. My gaze retraced the distance we had just walked, and I realised we had wandered a lot further than either of us had intended. I'd felt fine on the beach though. It was scaling the embankment that had done me in.

"Does your chest hurt?" Landon fretted, standing over me and scrutinising my face with anxious brown eyes. "Maybe I should call Roger and Troy. They'd come and pick you up, wouldn't they? I'm sure they wouldn't mind. I'll call them. Shall I? What do you think? Should I call them?"

"Jesus, Landon. No. You don't need to call them or anyone else. Just sit down and enjoy the view for five minutes. Then, once I get my breath back, we can walk home, even if it is very, very slowly.

"If you're sure..."

"I'm sure. Now sit."

He lowered his large frame onto the bench beside me and stared out at the choppy, grey water with a puzzled expression.

"Now what?" I asked, because it was obvious he had something else to say.

"Nothing. It's just..." He twisted around, so that he was facing the playing field. "If we're meant to be enjoying the view, shouldn't we be looking at the rugby players?"

CHAPTER 28

TWO WEEKS FLEW BY. Most evenings, Roger and Troy asked us have dinner with them. As a rule, they didn't provide evening meals for their guests, but they made an exception in our case, seeing as we were practically family anyway. That was what Roger said anyway. There were plenty of deep and meaningful conversations between the four of us. Sometimes, it was me with Roger, Landon with Troy. Other times, Troy would quietly pull me to one side while Roger spoke with Landon. And, sometimes, all four of us would sit and chat, with Landon and I trying desperately to absorb their words of wisdom in the hope we could learn how to make our relationship last for as long as theirs.

Our days were spent strolling along the beach or going by bus into Cardiff, or nearby Barry so that Landon could walk barefoot on the sand and dig his toes in to his heart's content.

Talking of hearts, mine seemed to grow stronger with every passing day. I found I was getting less out of breath on our walks or after climbing the stairs to our room. Sadly, my left arm showed little sign of improvement, even though

Landon stood over me and made sure I did my daily physio exercises.

What was probably even more annoying was Landon's stubborn refusal to have full on sex. We fooled around, much like we had done at Marcie's before our ill-fated date, but as soon as Landon considered I was getting too excited, he'd stop dead.

Wrong choice of words perhaps, because me ending up dead was exactly what he wanted to avoid. Still, it was frustrating. Landon was not to be budged on the matter, however much I wheedled and cajoled. If there had ever been a time when I thought the man to a pushover, he was determined to prove me wrong now.

Our last night found us, once again, sitting around the dining table with Roger and Troy.

Dinner had been a disgustingly healthy combination of jacket potato and steamed fish. Great for my heart, Landon's waistline and Roger's diabetes, but it did nothing for our taste buds and left us all still feeling hungry. Roger saved the day by producing a chocolate gateau that Troy didn't know he had hidden away.

"We're celebrating," Roger said with a self-satisfied smirk when Troy objected to the appearance of the chocolatey goodness. "The boys are young and healthy and at the beginning of their lives together. I say we raise a slice of chocolate cake and wish them well. May their journey on the path of true love be as long and as joyous as ours has been."

"Just this once then, you soppy old git," Troy muttered crossly, but I was sure I saw him wipe a tear from the corner of his eye.

"See? Compromise, boys," Roger said smugly. "That's what it's all about."

"Yeah?" Troy grumbled. "Funny how all our compromises are about me giving into you."

Roger shrugged. "But you love me anyway."

They smiled at each other in adoration and linked hands across the table.

Later, when the house was quiet and Landon and I were tucked up in our bed, I sighed heavily. Landon stirred sleepily.

"Are you okay? What is it? Chest pain?"

"No, nothing like that." I sighed a second time. "Actually, I suppose it is a bit like an ache in my heart."

"What?" Landon sat bolt upright, suddenly wide awake. He scrambled for the bedside lamp and I wasn't sure whether I should feel guilty or amused when I saw the look of sheer panic in his eyes. "Is it bad? What do I do? Who do I call?"

"Landon, relax. I'm not having a heart attack."

"But you said..."

"I know what I said." I sat up too, looking him straight in the eye. "The thing is, Landon, I want what they have so badly it hurts."

"I don't understand."

"Roger and Troy," I explained patiently. "I want what they have."

There was a long pause.

"You mean a guesthouse?"

"What the fuck? No, Landon!"

"Then...?" He blinked at me stupidly.

"I mean the kind of love they have. I want to spend the rest of my life loving just one person. I want to look at you in twenty or thirty years' time and feel the same way I feel about you now. I want you to feel that way too."

"You're sure it's me you want and not Stefan?" he asked in a small voice. Doubt clouded his beautiful eyes.

"One hundred percent," I said emphatically. "Make that one billion percent. I'll be honest, I'm always going to love Stefan, but as a friend, nothing more. I'm sorry I was such a dick about it before, but I swear, Landon, I didn't know what it was to really be in love with someone until I met you."

Landon's intense gaze searched my face, seeking the truth behind my words. Then he nodded.

"I feel like that too. I know we haven't been together for long, but you're it for me, Rufus. You're my one and only."

He reached for me, wrapping his arms around me and folding me into a massive bear hug. I snuggled against his chest, relishing the contact. But it wasn't enough. I wanted more. I wanted him inside me. I wriggled a hand beneath his t-shirt and gently squeezed the rolls of flesh I'd come to love so much. Flab, that a few months ago, would have turned me right off a guy. But this was Landon. He filled the void in my life that I hadn't even known was there until I met him. I adored him, love-handles and all. Actually... make that *especially* the love-handles.

Predictably, Landon pulled away and I groaned in frustration.

"I'm not sure we should..."

"Landon, it's been weeks. I promise you, nothing is going to happen. Nothing bad, anyway."

"I don't know, Rufus..."

"Look at it as our own personal commitment ceremony."

Landon's eyes widened.

"Are you... are you asking me to marry you?"

He was teasing me, the tell-tale quirk at the corner of his

mouth a dead giveaway. Maybe we hadn't been together for any great length of time, but it was long enough that I had come to know his moods. I knew when he was angry or sad or playful. And I definitely knew when his resolve was weakening and he was on the verge of giving in to me.

"Maybe, in a couple of years' time," I said, straight-faced, "we can do the fancy wedding thing like Stefan and Alex, but tonight is just for us. Kind of sealing the deal."

"And you swear you'll tell me if you start to feel funny."

"Is that a yes?" I grinned at him.

His answer was to push me down on to the mattress. He rolled on top of me, taking his weight on his arms. I spread my legs, letting him slide into the space between them. Slowly, he rubbed against me, creating a delicious friction, even through the material of our underwear.

Self-control didn't last. It had been too long for both of us. Impatience won out and in minutes we were both naked and Landon's fingers were inside me. The man might be sexually inexperienced compared to me, but he was a natural. He certainly knew what he was doing with those big fingers of his.

"Landon... please..."

He knew what I was asking for and he gave it to me, quickly replacing his fingers with the tip of his cock. I gripped his shoulders as he pushed into me slowly, his eyes on my face, searching mine for any signs of discomfort. Once his entire length filled me, he stilled, allowing us both a moment to adjust to the sensation.

When he began to move, I wrapped my arms around his neck, pulling his head down for a breathless kiss, and hooked my calves over his fleshy hips. My back arched, and I clawed at his back as his increasingly frantic thrusts deep-ened. Landon hissed sharply and dropped his head to my shoulder. His teeth bit into my sensitive skin and I groaned at the combination of pain and pleasure he was simultaneously giving me.

"Rufus... I don't... think I... can last..." Landon panted in my ear.

"Then don't. Come for me, baby."

Landon pushed a hand between our sweating bodies and grabbed my dick. His tugs were not in perfect synch with the snap of his hips, but close enough. We plunged over the edge and into a mind-blowing orgasm at the same, riding out the intense waves with guttural cries that the whole house must have heard. Not that I cared right at that moment.

I'd had better sex, sure, and with people who were better looking than Landon, but it had never meant as much as it did now, because I had never loved them the way I did him. Fact of the matter was, nobody had ever loved me that way either. Sex had always been like scratching an itch; a physical rather than an emotional need. Love had never been a requirement before, but Landon changed all that. He changed me.

Landon rolled onto his side and sighed contentedly. He rested one hand on my chest and I heard him counting under his breath. I rolled my head so that I was facing him.

"What are you doing?"

"Holding your heart," he said. "It's mine now. Always."

CHAPTER 29

MARCIE ARRIVED to pick us up the next morning, with Killigan in tow. They seemed so ridiculously happy and loved up, it verged on the point of being nauseating. And, okay, Landon and I were no different, but we were young and in the first throes of passion. They were old and had been together for years.

I pulled a face and rolled my eyes, earning myself a cuff around the back of the head from Roger and a disappointed look from Landon.

"I thought that's what you wanted for us," the latter of the two said quietly.

"Yeah, it is, but straight people are so... eughh!" I shuddered.

The second time is was Troy who slapped me, and a lot harder than Roger had.

"Ow!"

Marcic managed to put Killigan down for two seconds and turned to face us with raised eyebrows.

"Troy, did you just hit my darling Rufus?"

"I did indeed," Troy confirmed, totally unrepentant.

"Your darling Rufus needs to learn not to discriminate against people because of their sexuality."

"Hey, it's not for me to judge," I said piously. "I don't care what heterosexual people do behind closed doors. I just don't want to see it, that's all. I know they're straight. They don't have to shove it down my throat."

"*I'll* shove something down your throat," Landon teased. "That will shut you up."

I stared at him, shocked that he would say something like that in front of other people. Roger and Troy fell about laughing.

We loaded the bags into the car and then Landon and I left Marcie and Killigan to visit with Roger and Troy, while we took a last walk along the rocky beach.

Once we got back, it was hugs and kisses all round before we finally bundled into the car and set off for home. Marcie twisted around and shoved a hand between the seats, waving at Roger and Troy through the rear window like a mad woman. I found it a bit excessive and wondered what on earth she was playing at, until something on her finger suddenly glinted in the sunlight.

"Oh, my-fucking-God!" I squealed excitedly, grabbing her wrist and almost dragging her into the back seat.

"Jesus, Rufus!" Killigan swerved across the road. Luckily, there was no traffic coming the other way. "I'm driving here, you moron."

"But you're engaged!" I enthused, bouncing up and down on my seat as I studied the impressive rock on Marcie's finger. "I want to know everything. Who asked who? When's the wedding? How much did the ring cost? This is so exciting. We need to have a party. Please tell me we're having a party."

Marcie laughed, retracting her arm through the gap.

Killigan did his usual shaking his head and rolling his eyes, but he was smiling at the same time.

"I asked him," Marcie said. "He didn't answer at first. He went upstairs without a word and I thought I'd blown it, but then he came down with the ring." She smiled at Killigan fondly. "He'd had it since before your accident and was just waiting for the right time to pop the question. We haven't set a date yet, but we're planning on early next year. As for how much the ring cost, I really don't know."

"Not that it's any of your fucking business anyway," Killigan growled, glaring at me in the rear-view mirror.

"Language, Killigan!" Marcie slapped his arm. She didn't get told off for distracting him from driving, I noticed. "And, yes, there will a party. We're hiring out the whole of Franco's for the night. Rufus, we'd be honoured if you would do the cooking for us."

"Oh." Automatically, I covered my left hand with my right. "I want to. I'm just not sure that I can."

"You can do it, boy," Killigan said gruffly. "Alison said you can have free rein in the kitchen for the whole day and Franco will help."

"I'll help too," Landon offered. "I mean, I can't actually cook or anything, but there must be something I can do."

"You can help set up the dining room with Alison," Marcie suggested. "The boys are coming up from Weymouth, but Alex will go at it like a bull in a china shop and Stefan is going to do my hair. I'm sure Alison would appreciate you giving her a hand with the decorations."

Landon accepted happily, making me realise how much it meant to him to be included in our mismatched family. His own had abandoned him, yet he so badly wanted to belong somewhere. To *someone*. And, yes, he had me. We were committed to each other and looking forward to building something together, but Landon was the type of person who needed more. I didn't mind. Not that much anyway. I didn't doubt him when he said he loved me, but on the basis of no longer living my life as a selfish arsehole, I had to at least try and understand his need to have a family around him.

"Are Eric and Mason coming too?" I asked.

I wasn't sure how I would feel about that. I hadn't seen Eric since the accident. Marcie told me he had been there at the hospital while I was in the coma, but he and Mason had returned to the States before I woke. Obviously, Eric felt bad about setting me up with Donovan the way he had, and if I knew him at all, he'd feel guilty about the accident too. It was probable he blamed himself for what had happened. If he hadn't tried to split us up, Landon and I wouldn't have left the party when we did. We wouldn't have gotten into that stupid taxi. He hadn't tried to contact me since I'd been home, so I didn't know for sure. Maybe he hadn't called because he genuinely didn't give a shit. We'd have to have a talk at some point, but I wasn't sure I was ready to face him just yet.

"We'll invite them," Marcie said, "but I doubt they'll be able to come. It's not like Mason is going to cancel a tour date to come to a virtual stranger's engagement party, is he?"

It was easy to forget that Mason had never been one of Marcie's waifs and strays. He was a few years older than the rest of us for a start. He'd breezed into our lives and swept Eric off his feet, before carrying him off to America to act as the medic on Arcadia's tour. He'd never really been one of us, although I knew he got along with Alex and Stefan quite well. I didn't think he cared for me very much, but then who did other than Landon?

"Can we stop at the restaurant on the way home?" I asked. "I want to talk to Franco about the menu."

"Tell you what, we'll drop our better halves off at home and I'll come with you," Killigan said, shooting Marcie a sideways look.

"Don't you trust me?" I frowned, suspecting something was going on that I wasn't yet privy to. Whatever it was, I was sure I wasn't going to like it. Apart from Landon, nothing good ever happened to me.

"I want to talk to you about something, that's all."

I glanced at Landon anxiously. He shrugged and squeezed my hand.

"Don't worry," he mouthed silently.

But how could I not worry? Killigan had never been my biggest fan. Okay, he'd acted all concerned and fatherly when I was in the hospital, but that was when he thought I was dying. In the past, he'd pulled me aside for little chats plenty of times and usually they did not go well. For the rest of the journey home, I fretted over every possible scenario I could think of. In the end, I kept coming back to the what seemed like the most likely option. They had said Landon and I had a home with them for as long as we wanted, but that was before they decided to get married. What if they had changed their minds? I didn't blame them for wanting the house to themselves once they were newlyweds, but how were Landon and I supposed to afford anywhere to live on our crappy wages?

"You want us to move out, don't you?" I said, as soon as we alone in the car. I'd moved into the front passenger seat when we dropped Marcie and Landon off at the house.

"What? No, why would you think that?" Killigan sounded surprised.

"I don't know. Maybe because you don't like me much."

"Rufus, I like you just fine." Killigan sighed. "You've changed over the last few months. Other than your little relapse at the wedding, you've tried really hard to be a better person. We've all noticed it."

"Yeah, well..." I stared out of the window, suddenly embarrassed. "I guess you have Landon to thank for that."

"The old you wouldn't have looked twice at Landon," Killigan stated firmly. "This is all your own doing, Rufus. I'm proud of you, son. And... that's why I want you to be my best man."

My mouth dropped open in shock and I gawped at him like a brainless idiot. Actually, I had a brain, only it had ceased to function at this precise moment. Obviously, my hearing wasn't working that well either, because there was no way in hell I had heard him right. I was the last person on Earth he'd want standing beside him when he married Marcie.

"It's okay. You don't have to," Killigan said awkwardly, when I took too long to answer.

"No, it's just... I mean..." I floundered helplessly. "Fuck, I don't know what I mean. It's not that I don't want to, Killigan, but there must be someone else you could ask. There's Stefan, for a start. Or you must have friends at work you could ask."

"Oh God, Stefan! Can you imagine?" Killigan laughed and I found myself smiling too. "Marcie's already nabbed him to do her hair and make-up, anyway. And, yes, I have friends, but I don't want them. I want you."

"You're serious? You want me to be your best man?" I still couldn't quite believe this was happening, but my heart beat a little faster with excitement. Out of everybody he knew, he was choosing me. "Wait, don't you have a brother? Shouldn't you ask him?"

"Frankie, yes. He'll be at the wedding, but again – I'm not asking him, Rufus. I'm asking you. Now, will you please say yes and put me out of my misery?"

"Yes," I said. "Only if you're sure though. I mean... if you change your mind, I won't be offended."

Truth was, I would be. Hugely so. It only seemed fair to give him the option of backing out though.

"Rufus?"

"Yes?"

"Shut the fuck up."

CHAPTER 30

FROM WHERE I SAT, I could see every person who walked in, yet my heart still leapt into my throat each time the café door opened. I was the most nervous I had been in ages. Not because I was afraid that the person I was meeting with was going to harm me in any way, but because, potentially, she could hurt Landon. That was why I hadn't told him anything about this clandestine rendezvous.

In the two weeks we had been home from Wales, I'd gone from strength to strength. My left arm, while still far from perfect, had improved greatly with physio. I still tired easily if I overdid things, but I could use my arm again and had even put in a trial shift at the restaurant, with a view to starting back there on a part-time basis.

For the first time in my life, I was happy, reasonably healthy and feeling more confident since Killigan's bombshell request. Oh, and I was falling more and more in love with Landon with every passing day, which was why I did what I did. I'd thought a lot about Troy's story and the similarities to Landon's since we'd been home. I didn't want the same thing to happen to Landon. His parents were a lost cause, but maybe there was a chance he could still have a relationship with his sister.

Landon told me a while back, that she worked in an office block in Mayfair, so I tracked her down and called her. She was surprised to hear from me, but she agreed to meet without much persuasion.

She was late though, and I was on the verge of giving up on her when she breezed through the door. The first thing I noticed as she stood at the counter to order her drink, was the obvious swell of a baby-bump. I must have failed to hide my shock, because as she dropped into the chair opposite mine, she said, "Yes, I'm pregnant and yes... they threw me out too."

"Sorry," I told her with genuine concern. "Are you okay? Have you got some place to stay?"

"I'm with the baby's father. It's a shithole, but what can you do? I couldn't stay at home any longer. Not after they ordered me to have an abortion."

I raised my eyebrows. "Isn't that against their religion?"

"Only when it comes to other people." Sarah shook her head, as if it was too much to comprehend, even for her. "They tried to pray the gay away with Landon. Apparently, it's not as easy to pray away a baby."

"Didn't work that well with Landon either," I scoffed. "I think I'm living proof of that."

"I'm glad. I'd just discovered t I was pregnant when all of that awfulness happened. I knew my parents would kick me out once they found out. I also knew I couldn't leave Landon alone with them. You saved him, turning up when you did." She flashed me a sad smile. "How is he? I take it he doesn't want to see me as he's not here."

"He doesn't know," I confessed. "I wanted to talk to you

first. I had to be sure you weren't going to reject him and hurt him all over again."

"I wouldn't," she promised. "I won't. I want my brother in my life, Rufus. I want my child to know his Uncle Landie."

"Uncle Landie? Oh my God, he's going to love that!" I laughed.

"Do you really think so?" Sarah brightened noticeably at the thought, which made me believe she really did want to see Landon. "I'd like him to meet my boyfriend too. Or do you think it's too soon for that?"

"No, he'll want to, especially once he knows about the baby." I had a sudden brainwave; one of those things I probably should have discussed with Landon before blurting it out, but... too late. "Hey, why don't we have a double date? Let's go out somewhere. It'll be cool."

"Okay, maybe introducing them on neutral ground is a good idea. Did you have anywhere in mind?"

"Not really. It will have to be Thursday though. That's Landon's next night off."

"Thursday's good for me. I'm sure it will be for Rob too." She looked thoughtful for a moment. "How about that place on Cambourne Road? You know, the one that rock-star chap owns?"

"You mean Keane's?" I looked at her in surprise. "You know it's a gay bar, don't you?"

"So? I don't mind if you don't. I've never been to one before, especially not one owned by someone famous."

"I'm not sure it's a good idea," I said carefully. "It might not be the best place to take Landon."

"Why not? He's gay, isn't it?"

"Yes, but... let's just say, I know how bitchy the queens that go there can be."

Because I used to be one of them and not so long back either. My old friends – the ones who had pasted those hateful pictures to the windows of the restaurant – they went to Keane's. Landon may have lost some weight, but he was still big enough that they would torment him mercilessly. The fact he was with me wouldn't stop them. In fact, they would probably turn on me too, for what they would see as my betrayal to the cause. Twinks like us, we didn't give men who looked like Landon the time of day. We ridiculed them. Scorned them. No physical imperfections were tolerated in our pretty little world, even though most of us were not exactly perfect ourselves. I knew I'd changed and loved Landon for who and what he was, but it would be hard, putting myself back in that self-obsessed environment.

"You're ashamed of him," Sarah said, her eyes narrowing.

"No, I love him," I answered adamantly. "I just don't want to subject him to that if I don't have to."

She regarded me intently for a few moments longer.

"Is that a no to Keane's then?" Sarah sounded disappointed, even though I'd just told her it was Landon's own good that we didn't go there.

"Yes. I don't know... I suppose we could, if it's what you really want. Maybe it will be okay. They might not say anything if there's a few of us."

I doubted it somehow, but miracles did happen.

"Keane's it is then. Thursday night," Sarah said cheerfully. "I'll give you my number. This is just a suggestion, but what if you don't tell Landon I'm going to be there. Save it for a surprise."

I nodded reluctantly, thinking the whole thing was a bad idea. I was beginning to think I'd made a mistake in meeting up with her at all. She was bossy and demanding, just like her bloody mother, but she was still Landon's sister and he missed her. I didn't think she was a bad person. She was a victim of their parents too when it came down to it, but even so, she was thinking more of herself and what she wanted than the effect it would have on Landon.

"Fine, I'll get him there." I punched her number into my contacts list and gave her mine in return.

I left her to finish her drink and made my way home to an empty house. Everyone was still at work, so I went into the kitchen and searched the cabinets for something wild and wonderful to cook up for dinner. Marcie was the first to walk through the door, smiling in appreciation at the mouth-watering aromas coming from the pot on the stove.

"Can I borrow some money?" I said, once she had taken her coat and shoes off and settled at the kitchen table with a cup of coffee. "I want to take Landon out on Thursday night."

"I should think I can give you enough to take him some-where nice. Are you taking him anywhere special?"

"Um... I was thinking of going to Keane's."

"Sweetheart, are you sure that's a good idea?" Marcie asked, with justified concern.

"No, but we're meeting someone, and they chose Keane's, not me. Trust me, it's the last place I want to take Landon."

Marcie's attitude changed abruptly, as though someone had flipped a personality switch.

"Rufus Haynes, are you embarrassed to be seen with Landon?" she demanded. "Are you worried what your friends will say? Friends, I might add, who never came never anywhere near you while you were in the hospital."

"I don't care what they say about me," I told her

honestly. "I love Landon and if they don't like it, they can go fuck themselves."

"Lang…" Marcie began and then stopped herself. "Never mind. I'll let you have that one, because you're right."

"I just don't want them to upset Landon."

"Can't you ask this person if you can meet somewhere else?"

"It's Sarah," I said flatly. "Landon's sister."

"Ah, I see. Like mother, like daughter, is it?"

"She's not that bad, thank God. Just as bossy as fuck."

"Language!" Marcie slapped my arm. "You already had your free pass for today, so don't give me that look, young man."

"What look?" Landon asked, walking into the kitchen. "What's he done now?"

"Hey! You're supposed to be on my side." I laughed, sliding my arms around his ample waist and hugging him. It was always the best moment of my day when he got home from work. Today, he'd done the lunch time shift and had a few hours break before he had to be back for evening service. In a way, that was a good thing. Because it meant I got to welcome him home twice.

"I'm always on your side," he said, with a mischievous grin. "Marcie, what did he do?"

"Nothing that washing his mouth out with soap won't cure." Marcie threatened me with that all the time, Killigan too, who swore every bit as much as I did, if not more. So far, she hadn't done it to either of us, but I wouldn't put it past her. "He's also talking about taking you to Keane's," she added disapprovingly.

"Seriously?" Landon grin widened. "I've always wanted to go. When are we going?"

I could tell from Marcie's expression that it wasn't the reaction she expected.

"Thursday," I told him quickly, before she had a chance to tell him how much of a bad idea it was. "You can wear those purple panties for me."

"Fuck off!" Landon blushed furiously. "Not in front of Marcie."

"Hey, how come you didn't slap him for swearing?" I asked, as Marcie turned to leave the kitchen.

"Free pass," she called over her shoulder, and I heard her laughing the entire length of the hallway.

CHAPTER 31

THE CLUB WAS busy for a Thursday night. There were several faces I recognised, some of whom I'd probably slept with at some point. Who remembered that shit though? To be honest, when a person slept around as much as I had, the one-nighters tended to become one big blur. I didn't see any of my old friends though, which was something of a relief. We did get some funny looks as we made our way to the bar, but, thankfully, Landon was oblivious. He was enjoying himself, excited about being out on a proper date. And that was before he realised Sarah was there. I hoped seeing his sister would make his night rather than ruin it.

We got our drinks, beer for Landon and boring, old orange juice for me, because I was still watching the dodgy ticker. Then I pointed to a table near to the bar, where Sarah sat with a man who I assumed to be Rob, her boyfriend.

Landon's eyes widened and he rushed over to his sister, only remembering at the last second to put his drink down before he pulled her into a giant hug that took everyone by surprise. Because of the way their mother was, I never imagined Landon to have a tactile relationship with his sister. Then again, Sarah seemed as startled by it as I was, so maybe it was a new thing.

"I can't believe you're here," Landon enthused, when he finally released her. "Does Mother know? Who's this? And... oh my word... you're pregnant!"

"Mother threw me out too," Sarah told him, as we all sat down at the table. "It seems as though an illegitimate grandchild is no more welcome in their home than a homosexual son."

"You don't need them," Landon said firmly, although the look on his face suggested he still wished things were different with his parents. "You will always have Rufus and I to support you." He glanced at Sarah's boyfriend. "I assume you're the father?"

"Yes, I'm Rob. Pleased to meet you at last."

He held his hand out across the table. Landon hesitated before he shook it, presumably because he was unaccustomed to people being friendly and accepting, without judgement from the outset.

I admired that about Rob. He obviously wasn't fazed by either Landon's size or sexuality, or by the fact he found himself in a gay nightclub. Other than that, he was fairly ordinary. Average height, average build. Even his facial features were what one might call nondescript. He seemed nice enough though and that was all that mattered if he was going to spend any time around Landon.

"Rufus, what the fuck is this?"

My heart sank as I looked up into the sneering face of Seb. Louis stood behind him, smirking. Beside me, Landon tensed. I knew he recognised them from the night they had humiliated him in the restaurant.

"No wonder nobody has seen you around lately," Seb

continued, his gaze raking over Landon with evident distaste. "I'd be ashamed to go out in public too, if that fat walrus was the only thing I could pull."

"Hold on," Louis said over Seb's shoulder. "Isn't that the jelly-belly from that shitty restaurant you work in?"

Sarah and Rob looked on in shock, but neither of them up spoke up in Landon's defence. Feisty as she was, I'd expected Sarah to go in, all guns blazing if anyone said anything to her brother, but she didn't move. Landon sat with his head bowed, shoulders hunched. My heart broke for him a little.

I got to my feet and squared up to Seb. He was roughly the same height as me, so I was able to look him straight in the eye. I did something I had never done before. I stood up for myself. For Landon. For love.

"I never thanked you for that, did I?" I said, with a cold smile.

Blank faces stared back at me. I wasn't worried about the situation descending into a fist fight. At the end of the day, Seb and Louis were still the way I used to be. Shallow, self-centred, bitchy little queens, obsessed with image. Cowards. If Landon stood up, they would probably shit their panties on the spot.

"Thank us for what?" Seb asked, perplexed.

"Well, if you hadn't been so bloody awful to Landon that night, I might never have seen you for the spiteful pricks you really are. I also wouldn't have got to know Landon and I would have missed out big time. So that's what I'm thanking you for. He's the best thing that ever happened to me. I love him with every fibre of my being. So suck on that, Sebastian, and then piss off."

"Fuck you!" Seb spat furiously, obviously at a loss for anything more intelligent to say.

"No, thanks. Been there, done that. To be blunt, Landon is a million times better."

I sat back down, surprised when the tables nearest to ours burst into a round of applause and cheered. Shame-faced, Seb and Louis turned tail and ran, disappearing into the crowd. I paid them no more attention, turning to face Landon instead, who was staring at me in amazement. Sarah and Rob stared too, but I didn't really care what they thought of my behaviour.

"Sorry," I mumbled to Landon, guessing he probably didn't think much of me now that he knew I'd slept with Seb. Even though it had happened ages ago, Landon wouldn't like hearing about it.

"What on Earth are you sorry about?" Sarah exclaimed. "You really gave them what for. It was brilliant."

"Thanks, but..." I didn't take my eyes from Landon. Giving Seb and Louis what for wasn't what I was apologising for. Landon understood that, even if nobody else did.

"You love me," Landon said.

"You know I do. I've told you enough times."

"Yes, but now you've shown me." He glanced down at the table, suddenly awkward. "And thanks for saying I'm better than him, even though I know it's not true."

"Says who? Landon, you are the best I've ever had. Maybe it's because I feel more for you than anyone else I've been with, but sex with you actually means something for the first time in my life."

"And that's enough of that," Sarah interrupted. "Honestly, I don't need to hear about my little brother's sex life."

"Excuse me, unless that's the immaculate conception, you've been at it too," Landon scoffed, making us all laugh.

Pop. Pop pop. I turned my head, trying to pinpoint the strange sound I'd heard over the music. Landon didn't seem to notice. Nor did Sarah and Rob, but a few people at other tables craned their necks too, trying to see what was going on.

Pop pop. Pop pop. That was when the screaming started. The music cut out abruptly and the popping noise suddenly became loud bangs. Now people noticed. Panic reigned as they ran in all directions, falling over each other and trampling those already on the floor.

A quick-thinking barman threw open the door that led to the stock room and the rear entrance of the club. Those nearest to the door and the ones not to blinded by fear to recognise the escape route, rushed in that direction. Fights broke out as they all tried to push through the doorway at the same time.

And I just sat there. My brain screamed at me to run, but my whole body was frozen in place. I couldn't think. Could barely even breathe. Through a gap in the milling club-goers, I saw the shooter, a man no older than me. Cold dead eyes met mine and the gunman smiled. He raised the gun, aiming it directly at me. Then the gap closed and I don't know if he fired or not, but I felt a hot trickle of urine dampened the crotch of my trousers.

"Rufus! Rufus, we need to go. Please."

I blinked, turning tear-filled eyes in the direction of the voice. Landon. He was still there. He should have run. Why hadn't he run?

"Rufus, please."

"I... I can't... I..."

Bang. Bang. A man dropped to the floor, close to where Landon stood, eyes staring sightlessly at the ceiling. *Bang.* Landon flinched. Blood blossomed on the sleeve of his shirt. I stared in horror, but still couldn't make my legs work. I was going to die, I knew it. And, if Landon didn't leave, he would die too.

"Landon, go. Leave me."

"Never."

Landon stooped. Grabbing me around the waist, he picked me up and threw me over his shoulder.

Bang. Something whistled past my ear. Landon ran. Not towards the back door, where human traffic clogged the corridor, with those at the back making neat little targets for the gunman, but the other way. Towards the main entrance of the club. By some miracle, the shooter didn't fire at us again.

Moments later we spilled out onto a street ablaze with flashing blue lights. Sirens blared and people rushed everywhere. Landon set me down on the kerb. A paramedic hurried over to us and armed police stormed into the club. It was only later that the speed of their response struck me. The events inside Keane's lasted less than five minutes, but for reasons we would never know, the gunman had phoned the police on his way to the club and told them where he was and what he was about to do. That was why they had reached us as quick as they had. The gunman had charged at them as they entered the club. He had been shot dead on the spot. Killigan called it suicide by police.

Thankfully, Rob had gotten Sarah out as soon as he realised what was happening. Landon's wound was minor. The bullet had only grazed his arm rather than piercing the flesh. Still, he was one of the lucky ones. Seventeen people were shot that night, some of them receiving life-changing injuries. Seven people lost their lives, including my old friend Louis. I might not have liked him much in the end, but he didn't deserve to die.

My life changed too. I hadn't been shot. Hadn't been

injured. I simply stopped living. Oh, I still breathed and walked and talked, but I shut myself in my bedroom and refused to see anyone. Not even Landon. How could I look him in the eye when it was my fault he had been hurt? It was my indecisiveness, my inability to save myself that almost got him killed. Even if Landon forgave me, I could never forgive myself.

And I couldn't go outside. Not ever again. Not while where there were people out there who wanted me dead because of who I chose to love.

So, I hid myself away from the world. Safe in my own private little bubble.

In short, Rufus Bartholomew Haynes ceased to exist.

CHAPTER 32

TIME PASSED. I didn't know how much. Days. Weeks. I didn't care. I scuttled to the bathroom and back whenever I needed to piss, but only ever when there was nobody else around. The whole time I was out of my room, my heart hammered against my ribcage and my limbs shook. I found it almost impossible to breathe until I was back in the safety of my room. Marcie brought my meals up for me and left them outside my door. Some I ate. Some I didn't.

Different people came to my door, pleading with me to speak to them. My mum and dad, Marcie, Killigan, Landon, Stefan, Eric, even Troy and Roger. Eric told me through the door that Mason was home too. It was his club after all, so I guess he had enough of his own shit to sort out. It destroyed me to turn them away, especially Landon, but I just couldn't do it. What if I let them in and something happened to them because of me? Because I was weak and stupid and didn't deserve to live in the first place?

There was one person though, who was never going to take no for an answer. I should have known he would only wait for so long before taking matters into his own hands. I just never imagined he actually cared enough about me to do it.

"Knock knock. Coming in. Like it or not."

"Go away, Alex." As usual, I was on my bed, lying on my side and staring at the wall. Worse than watching paint dry, I was literally watching dry paint.

"Can't do that, Doofus." Alex-bloody-Gill dropped onto the end of my bed, forcing me to tuck me knees up and give him space. Either that or he'd sit on my feet anyway and then complain they were too bony and digging in his arse. "You and me need to talk."

I sighed, my soul too weary to put up a fight, even with Alex. "Why would they send you up, of all people?"

"They wouldn't," he answered, patting my leg like I was a damn puppy or something. "In fact, I'm under strict instructions to stay the fuck away from you. But you know what, I'm not going to. Whatever shit went down between us in the past. I fucking hate seeing you like this."

"You think I want to be like this?" The tears started once more, and I couldn't stop them. I let them flow down my face, unchecked. I didn't even have the energy to raise a hand to my face and wipe them away. "I'm trying so hard, Alex. I wake up every morning and I think, 'today is the day I get my life back'. And then I can't fucking move. Or I go to the bathroom and after, I stand at the top of the stairs, telling myself, it's not that much further. Just one step at a time. But I can't do it. I fucking can't. I..."

"Hey, come here." To my surprise, Alex reached over and hoisted me bodily into his lap. He wrapped his big, strong arms around me tightly. I didn't resist. It felt good to be held. Safe. Even if it was the wrong man. "Don't tell Stef about this. I always tell him tears don't work on me."

"Do you ever wonder if it's worth it?" I whispered against his massive chest.

"If what's worth it?"

"This. Us. The way we are." I sniffed and wiped my nose on his t-shirt. In normal circumstances he would have killed me for getting snot on him, but we were way beyond normal already. "Being gay."

"Rufus, you know who I was before I met Stef," Alex said, shifting his weight beneath me. "I tried to fight it, my attraction to him, because I didn't want to be gay. But in the end, I had to accept it. It's who I am. And when I look at Stef, I don't regret one damn thing we went through to be get where we are now. So, yeah... it's worth it."

"But you were stabbed and left for dead for being gay. Stefan was kidnapped and drugged by his own father because he's gay. Landon and all those people... they were shot for being gay. It's too much. I don't... I don't think I can do it anymore."

"Rufus, it doesn't work like that. You can't just stop being gay."

"I know, but..."

"So, what? Are you saying you don't love Landon?"

"No, I do, but... it's my fault he was hurt," I sobbed. "If I hadn't taken him to Keane's..."

"You want to know something? I felt the same way when Stef got that scar on his leg. I blamed myself, but do you know what he said? He said it wasn't me who petrol-bombed his flat. Same goes for you. It wasn't you who took a loaded gun into a nightclub and shot a bunch of people. That fucking prick would have done it whether you were at Keane's or not. Landon doesn't blame you. He went to that club with you. His choice. So, give yourself a break and go talk to your boyfriend. He's worrying himself sick about you."

I put one hand on his chest and pushed myself upright. "I'm scared."

"You don't have to be. There's a lot of people downstairs who love you. And, don't forget you still have an engagement party to cater. Nobody is going to hurt you, Rufus."

"Will... will you come with me?"

"If you want me to, yeah."

Even with Alex's encouragement, it still took another fifteen minutes before I could bring myself to leave the sanctuary of my bedroom. Really, I needed a shower and a shave before facing decent company, but Alex wouldn't let me. He claimed if I stopped to clean up, I would lose my momentum and not make it as far as down the stairs at all. Strange and new as it was to agree with Alex over anything, I knew he was right. I'd chicken out the first chance I got.

Alex went down the stairs in front of me. I followed tentatively behind, clinging on to the back of his t-shirt with one hand. He walked into the living room, clearing his throat to get the attention of everyone gathered. I could see that everyone was shocked by my appearance. Stefan's eyes darted to where my hand connected to Alex and he raised his eyebrows. They all moved towards me at once and I felt the panic surge in my chest. If not for Alex grabbing my wrist, I would have turned and run back up to my room, but he wouldn't let me.

"Okay, give him space," Alex growled, and the advance stopped in their tracks, although each of them eyed me hungrily as though they couldn't wait to get their hands on me. "Landon, I guess you get to go first."

"Hold on a minute," Dad said crossly. "Rufus is our son.

Who the hell are you to give orders about who can and can't go near him?"

"Alex is our resident macho idiot and all-round tough guy," Killigan told him. "Come on, I'll get you another beer."

"And I'll make more tea." Marcie smiled at my mother. "Claire, would you mind helping me? Stefan, Eric, you can come too. Roger, Troy... let's give the boys five minutes alone."

Everyone filed out of the room, until there was only Landon and I remaining. He stood over by the window, watching me through hooded eyes. He made no move towards me. The trust had gone. I'd hurt him far more by pushing him away than the gunman had by shooting him. If I was to blame for anything, it was shutting him out when he needed me. Landon had to be scared and traumatised too, and I'd let him go through it alone when we should have been together. If he didn't hate me for taking him to Keane's that night, he had to hate me for abandoning him directly after.

"I'm sorry."

"I know." He walked over to the sofa and perched on the end cushion. "I don't blame you, Rufus, for what happened. And I get that you needed to shut yourself away for a while. I'm not angry with you about that either."

"Then what are you angry about?" I sat on the other end of the sofa, watching his face closely. "Because there's something, I can tell."

"You left me, Rufus. You said you loved me and then you left me."

"I didn't go anywhere," I protested weakly. "I was right upstairs the whole time."

"Right upstairs and totally unreachable," Landon

snorted. "You wouldn't let me see you. You might as well have been on the other side of the world."

"I didn't... I didn't mean to leave you."

"But you did it anyway."

"I know. I really am sorry." Silently, I pleaded with him to look at me, but he kept his gaze fixed firmly on the floor. "Landon, I... shit, it's hard to explain."

"Try."

"I wanted to see you. To talk to you and touch you. But... I don't know... I *couldn't*. My brain, my body... they just wouldn't do as I asked. Every day, I thought I could do it, but... I was so scared, Landon. Scared that you would hate me. Scared that if I went outside, something would happen. To me, to you. If you want the truth, I'm still scared. There's people out there who want to kill me... kill *us*... because of who we are."

Landon looked up. He twisted around on the sofa so that he faced me.

"I'm scared too, Rufus. That night at Keane's, I saw him point that gun at you. You just sat there. And that's what I see, over and over again. You, sitting there." Landon wiped his eyes on his sleeve. "I thought I was going to lose you."

"You saved me."

"And then I lost you anyway."

"No, I'm right here, Landon."

"You're not though, are you? You pushed me away."

Turning to the side, I hugged my knees to my chest and rested my chin on top of them. I began to cry again. Landon stared at me, torn between holding onto his anger and forgiving me.

"It wasn't just you," I mumbled through my tears. "I pushed everyone away."

"Everyone except Alex!" Landon exploded, leaping to his feet. "Why would you let him in and not me?"

That was the real reason he was angry with me? He was jealous because he thought I'd let Alex into my room rather than him? I guess, on some level, it made sense, because he'd known from the start how much I had always disliked Alex.

"Uh, hello..." I said, lifting my head from off my knees and watching him pace angrily up and down in front of the sofa. "Have you met Alex? You do know I never had a say in the matter?"

"No, I suppose not." Landon sighed heavily and sat down again; a cushion closer to me than before which was progress. "It's not fair though."

"No, it's not and I'm sorry," I said again. Cautiously, I slithered one leg forward until my bare foot rested against his thigh. He glanced down with a frown, but he didn't shove my foot away. "But maybe his bull-headed approach was what I needed to get my arse in gear. Alex is the only one who didn't actually go away when I told him to."

"So now it's my fault?"

"No, I'm not saying that. You gave me space when I needed it and I'm grateful that you did. I don't know, Landon. Maybe it was time for me to return to the land of the living and Alex just happened to be there to nudge me in the right direction."

"Maybe," Landon conceded grudgingly. Subconsciously, he dropped a hand to my foot and began to massage my toes. I didn't say anything, in case he realised what he was doing and stopped. "It still hurts though, that he got through to you when I couldn't."

"But it's not like he kept me for himself," I said lightly. "He gave me straight to you."

Landon smiled.

"Makes you sound like a birthday present."

"Yeah?" I nudged him with my foot. "Want to unwrap me?"

"Not until you've had a shower and got rid of those whiskers." Landon wrinkled his nose in distaste. "Plus, you need to speak to your parents and Marcie and Killigan. Stefan's been going mental too. They all need to see that you're okay."

"I'm not sure I am okay, Landon. Not yet."

"You will be though," Landon said with a certainty I wished I could share. "It's still in the process of being sorted, but Mason is setting up a fund to help the survivors and–"

"I don't want Mason's money, Landon." Christ, I really had changed. Even I never thought the day would come when I turned down free money. "I just want to get better."

"But that's what the fund is for. To provide counselling and whatever support we need to get through this."

"You're getting help?"

"Yes. My first appointment is Friday. I'm messed up too, Rufus. Everybody is who was there that night."

"I'll think about it. Is that okay for now?"

"One day at a time, Rufus. That's all any of us can do."

He shifted closer, lifting my legs so that after a moment or two of manoeuvring, I was sat on his lap, his arms around my waist. I rested my head on his shoulder and closed my eyes. All I could think was how fucking stupid I had been, wasting so much time in my bed and wallowing in self-pity. Missing out on being held in the loving arms of my boyfriend.

"Are you ready to see the others yet?" he asked.

"In a minute. Can we stay here, like this, for a while first?"

"Whatever you want."

"Landon?"
"Yes, Rufus?"
"Hold my heart."
Landon laid his hand in my chest.
"Always," he said.